ADVANCE PRAISE FOR

Stir It Up!

"Laurie brings out the creativity and joyful child in everybody. Reading her welcome to *Stir It Up!* and the stories that go with each exercise inspires me to access my playful side. Play brings color, flavor, dimension, depth and honesty to work tasks. These are great exercises for bringing people together and helping them work innovatively. Thanks for making these available, Laurie!"

> —**Dr. Sharon Livingston,** President, Sharpen The Focus Institute, Inc.
> School for Qualitative Research

"*Stir It Up!* does just what it promises to do—stirs up the way researchers moderate or facilitate groups. Drawing on her love of cooking, Laurie Tema-Lyn provides a wonderful collection of "recipes" for changing the dynamics of groups and getting to a deeper level of insights. As a reader, there's so much to choose from. Researchers can build the techniques into their guides or have them in their back pocket, ready to use when we run into trouble (a listless focus group, a guarded interviewee, for instance). These are recipes we can adapt to our situations and, most importantly, to our personalities and moderating styles. Thanks, Laurie!"

> —**Judy Langer,** Langer Qualitative

"If *Stir It Up!* were a restaurant it would receive a 5 Star rating. I can't stop thinking about all of the creative ideas and techniques presented throughout the book. A must have for QRC professionals, especially anyone leading ideation or brainstorming sessions. I am even working a few of these techniques into a current discussion guide."

> —**Jim Berling,** SVP, Burke, Inc.

"Laurie's *Stir It Up!* is sure to bring rich, flavorful learning to any focus group (or dining room) table. The easy-to-use nature of each technique and of the book itself will make *Stir It Up!* one of the most dog-eared and worn books on your research shelf. Discussion guides and meeting agendas will be so much more exciting to draft; the dialogues themselves so much more fruitful. A wonderful means of energizing any qualitative research discussion!"

—**Alissa Jaquish,** Sr. Manager, Customer Insights,
Southwest Airlines

"Laurie Tema-Lyn's *Stir It Up!* is, as its subtitle implies, a "cookbook" for innovation. The exercises are carefully explained and well thought out, and like an excellent cookbook, guarantee results every time. As innovation continues to be an ingredient essential to corporate success, Tema-Lyn's clever exercises provide a way of optimizing new product development meetings. Her ideas are refreshing and entertaining and will stimulate discussion long after the ideation session is over."

—**Marcia Mogelonsky**, Ph.D., Global Food Analyst
Mintel International

"Laurie's 'cookbook' is a gift, destined to become a resource for novices and as well as seasoned chefs in the art of facilitating focus groups, meetings, or events. While *Stir It Up!* provides recipes of ingredients and process steps, it paradoxically and masterfully invites, inspires and convinces us to use our own powers of creativity and spontaneity."

—**Patricia Sunderland,** Partner, Practica Group, LLC

Stir It Up!

Recipes for Robust Insights & Red Hot Ideas

Laurie Tema-Lyn
Practical Imagination Enterprises®

Nancy

It was a pleasure to work with you! Wishing you much success on Toys!

Laurie 11/9/16

PMP

Paramount Market Publishing, Inc.

Paramount Market Publishing, Inc.
950 Danby Road, Suite 136
Ithaca, NY 14850
www.paramountbooks.com
Voice: 607-275-8100; 888-787-8100
Fax: 607-275-8101

Publisher: James Madden
Editorial Director: Doris Walsh

Library of Congress Catalog Number available
Cataloging in Publication Data available
ISBN 978-0-9830436-3-8

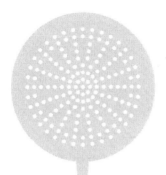

Dedicated to my Mom, Jeanne Carlin, the first encourager,

and one who liked to "stir up the pot" . . . and to all those

who want to nurture inspiration, insights, and great ideas.

Contents

PREFACE

It started just before Thanksgiving 2010. Research colleague Amy asked me to help her with activities for getting insights and ideas to incorporate in an upcoming project. Before we parted she asked, "Isn't there a good book for this?"

At 3 a.m. that morning I decided it was time to start writing it!

Acknowledgements

This book would not be possible without the positive energy, encouragement, and wise counsel of so many:

To my husband Ron, for his loving patience, humor, faithful review, and critique.

To dear friend and frequent collaborator Reva Dolobowsky, first line editor and advisor.

To family cheerleaders—Dad, Shari, Steve, Ian and Samara, and to Rachel, whose kitchen table was the place where the first exercises were drafted in the wee hours of the morning.

To Judy Langer, Tom Asacker, and Paul Marciano for publishing advice.

To friend and lawyer Eleanor Uddo.

To my book name council: Deb VanDeWeghe, Lisa Parker, Gayle Jay, Bruce Duhan, Jacquie Ottman, Cathy Davis, and Patti Sunderland.

To Harvey and Eileen Ehrlich for support throughout and to Harvey for his thousands of marvelous illustrations in projects we've done through a long history together.

To Steve DeCanio for the lovely photo.

To author coach Joel Orr.

To my furry pals Mr. Buttons and Imp who relax and inspire me.

And I am grateful to Paramount Market Publishing: James Madden and Doris Walsh who said, "Yes!"

INTRODUCTION

Open a great cookbook and you enter a world of ideas—ingredients, tools, and techniques that can create mouth-watering, eye-delighting, palate-pleasing creations.

This is a "cookbook" of sorts—it's chock full of tools and techniques to use whenever you are looking to stir up *something new* (like ideas), *something deep* (like insights), *something exciting* (like good energy and teamwork). It's designed to be used and abused by meeting practitioners, qualitative market researchers, or just about anyone on a quest for insights or ideas.

The intention in writing out exercises in this form is to make the *new*, easy to do. But I'm not suggesting that you slavishly follow the recipes. Use them as guides, as sparks, until you feel comfortable, then make them your own with your unique variations. Most of my work with consumers and client teams is done in person, so you will see that I've written the exercises in a conversational tone. While my frequent tools are flip chart and markers, pen and paper you will find that many of these activities are adaptable to an online platform. If online is your primary mode of working, you will have to experiment to find exactly the right words and symbols that convey in text what is more easily communicated through body language, tone of voice, and other non-verbals. And just like any creative enterprise, if something doesn't work exactly the way you anticipated see what you've learned from this—or just move on to another activity.

I hope you will bring the book to the field, to the boardroom, to the focus group. Put your notes and sticky notes in it. If the book gets messy I will have done my job! Try out the exercise recipes. See what tastes good to you and those you've gathered in your midst. Make notes of what you do; and what yields good results.

The book is organized in five sections:

Ice Breakers or Warm Up Exercises are just that. Use them at the beginning

Ice Breakers, Truthsayers, Energy Changers, Connection-Makers, and Idea Developers of a group discussion to get people relaxed and comfortable and to set the stage for the type of gathering you intend to hold.

Truthsayers are primarily for use in qualitative research settings. They are designed to help develop robust insights into the hearts, minds, and experiences of research participants—whether you define them as consumers, product or service users, shoppers, or sophisticated professionals.

Energy Changers are activities to fuel or recharge a group, or to guide participants into quiet reflection.

Connection-Makers are the heart of idea generation. These exercises use the senses and a variety of different thinking styles. Among the tools are analogy, metaphor, intuition and empathy.

Idea Developers are activities to select preliminary ideas and directions, and add more detail to prepare them for next steps like concept evaluation or prototype creation.

A Bit of Theory

As you can see, the emphasis here is on pragmatism rather than theory. There are many outstanding books and articles on creativity, and how the brain works to produce connections and ideas. When I first started in the innovation consulting business, the theories of Roger Sperry, who won the Nobel Prize in 1981 for his work on understanding how the brain functions, were cutting edge. We consultants all spoke of the differentiation between right and left hemispheres of the brain. The right side was deemed the center of our creative, artistic, and intuitive processes and the left (the logical side) described as the seat of our analytical, rational brains.

Researchers these days have expanded beyond the split-brain theory to speak more of the *neuroplasticity* of the brain and the ability for different parts of the brain to be able to reallocate the real estate and take over functions if one part is damaged.[1]

The theorists supporting "intelligent memory" suggest that analysis and intuition work collaboratively in the mind in all modes of thought so that there really is not a differentiation between "left brain" and "right brain."[2] Eric Kandel won the Nobel Prize in 2000 for his contribution to this work.

1. William Duggan, Booz & Company, "How Aha! Really Happens," in *Strategy+ Business,* Issue 61 Winter 2010.

2. Brenda Milner, Larry Squire, and Eric Kandel. "Cognitive Neuroscience and the Study of Memory," in the journal *Neuron,* describing a new model of the brain, 1998.

This new model negates previous thinking and shows that there is learning and recall, in various combinations, throughout the entire brain. Our brains are stocked with shelves of information and memory based on what we've seen, heard, experienced or read about before. The creative "ahas!" take place when we have "presence of mind"—in other words, when we clear our brains of expectations, so that we can search our information or memory storage banks and make unique connections through stimulating questions.

The activities in this book are varied, and tap into our **whole brains.** In my 25 years' experience as consultant and researcher they have been proven to work.

How to Use this Book

The exercises are designed to be user-friendly and foolproof. Each one identifies the type of exercise, degree of difficulty, number of participants, approximate timing, and materials needed. *Tips, watch-fors,* and *stories* are sprinkled within each section and activity.

The "scripts" are *suggestions* for ways to position and direct the exercises. Of course, you should use your own language and style. Think of these activities as more akin to making a delicious, colorful salad than a from-scratch cake where precise measurements are called for.

A note about the "Codes"

The upper right hand corner includes the type of exercise; and some can be used for multiple purposes. *Time* provides a guideline about how much time you are likely to spend doing the activity in a session. Of course, it can vary widely depending upon your style, the assembled team and the situation. There is also a guideline about degree of difficulty.

Elsewhere in the text of most of the exercises are more details.

Time is broken down into:

Set Up Time, meaning your instructions and preparing the team to do the exercise;

Run Time gives an idea about how much time it will take for participants to do the activity; and

Sharing is the additional time that participants will spend talking through their responses with the full assembled group.

Materials

For the majority of the exercises the basic tools are note pads and writing implements for participants; flip chart paper and markers for facilitators. Special materials are noted as well.

Team Size

For consumer groups this is often 6 to 8 participants, although I occasionally work with smaller or larger numbers. Client team sessions typically range from 8 to 12 people, although occasionally we work with much larger groups. I've given a range for most of the activities.

And, Finally

Both art and science are needed to pull these exercises off successfully. The "art" rests on your shoulders as moderator/facilitator/coach. Approach your facilitation with useful attitudes: a dose of experimentation, playfulness, spontaneity, humor, and trust in successful outcomes, and you will produce those results. Pay attention to what happens when you employ an activity and record it—that's why the worksheets are built into the book, so you can reflect back and learn from your experiences. Don't get dismayed if something occasionally misfires; just be sure you have other options to pull out of your back pocket. As the author Henry Miller said, *"All growth is a leap in the dark, a spontaneous unpremeditated act without benefit of experience."*

I wish you great success as you take that leap!

ICE BREAKERS

Dear Readers,

Welcome. I'm glad you have found this book. Pull up a comfy chair and let's have a little chat. Imagine that I've got a nice fire going in the fireplace; you can hear it crackling; it's warm and cozy here. Perhaps you can smell the delicious aroma of the spicy tomato vegetable soup warming on the stove. I'll tell you a little about my story and me and I hope to get to know you and your story.

My name is Laurie Tema-Lyn; my company is Practical Imagination Enterprises. I am passionate about my work. As a creative catalyst and qualitative market research consultant I engage people in conversations about their hopes, desires and experiences. I listen deeply and without judgment. My role is to help people stretch their thinking and use their imagination to come up with ideas and solve thorny problems—whether for new strategies, or products that make life a bit easier, or new ways of communicating the benefits of products and services. I love what I do and I love to share it with others. I live in a pre-Revolutionary War home in a semi-rural community in central New Jersey, not far from Princeton. Sharing my home are my story-teller husband, our dog and cat, and a mysterious number of koi fish in the small pond outside our living room door.

There you have it. I've demonstrated an Ice Breaker or a warm up exercise. I've told you a little about myself, and perhaps you've gathered some clues about how I live and what I value.

I believe that just as the way you welcome a friend into your home with a smile and words to set them at ease, when you conduct a meeting of any type, the same principles hold true.

As researchers and consultants you know that the first few minutes are critical for setting the tone and expectations for a discussion with one person or many. Some even say that we are drawn to people in the first three

Activities to get people relaxed and comfortable and to set the stage for the work to come

seconds, hence the phrase, "snap judgments." But aside from setting a warm and friendly tone, Ice Breakers do many other things:

- They help participants get comfortable talking; speaking aloud in a group, particularly of strangers, is not so easy for everyone.

- We quickly learn a bit about each other and see where we may have common experiences that we can build upon and relate to.

- In a research setting, attentive moderators and back-room listeners can find that important clues about research subjects' attitudes, behaviors and values are likely to be hinted at very early in the process, even before we get into the heart of the research discussion.

- Ice Breakers help set the stage for Individuals to coalesce into Teams.

- And we can use very specific Ice Breaker exercises to provide a mental framework for the type of discussion or idea session that we want.

For the most part, Ice Breaker exercises are relatively brief and easy to do; but occasionally you get thrown a curve ball, and have to be fast on your feet to redirect the exercise.

This happened to me recently. I provided the welcoming and was charged with conducting the first portion of a professional meeting. As this was the night after the Oscar awards show I asked my colleagues—some of whom I've known for years, to introduce themselves and say a little about a movie character that they identify with in some way. I demonstrated and mentioned that I was impressed with the young woman in *True Grit* for her clarity of purpose, fearlessness, and ability to engage and persuade others to action. After my statement, I turned to the person on my left who thought a moment and said she hadn't been to movies in ages and couldn't come up with a response. Her comment was echoed by many. Surprised, but not panicked; I opened the door wider to movies from the past or even literary characters, and the exercise proceeded with each member offering an interesting and thoughtful contribution. The Ice Breaker, though it didn't work exactly as I had anticipated, still worked. Everyone participated, each person's voice was heard, I learned a bit more about old friends and newcomers, and we set the tone for the meeting. Everyone saw that it was not going to be a passive lecture experience, but one in which we would draw upon personal experiences to generate ideas.

The following pages offer a range of Ice Breaker exercises, from ones that are very easy to do, to others that require some preparation or teaching.

For all these activities, there are a few simple guidelines to keep in mind:

Model your response first. As moderator/facilitator I feel strongly that you have to add something of yourself to the conversation if you want to have people comfortable in sharing their stories. I'm not suggesting you reveal intimate details of your life, but say something that is both personal and true. Modeling is also important in terms of time management. If your intro is brief, the rest of the group is likely to follow suit.

Go from "safe" or simple to more revelatory. If you are working with a group for a while you might ask people to tell you "the food they eat in secret," but that's not the first activity I would ask people to talk about. Start simple, with a verbal Ice Breaker, gain their trust, and then you can engage participants in more revealing conversation or activities like drawings or role-plays.

Accept whatever participants offer you and thank them so that they know they have been heard and valued. As in my Oscar exercise, my teammates came up with responses that I hadn't imagined. I redirected the activity, opened the window wider so that they had more room for their responses, and thanked them.

But most important is your attitude. An Ice Breaker is an invitation to engage, to dance, and to play. It should set the stage for a dynamic that encourages communication and will be pleasurable and productive for your participants and for yourself. Offer your Ice Breakers with confidence in your group and in yourself, and you'll be off to a great start!

The Story of Your Name

This is a fascinating introductory exercise. It can reveal a lot about the participants in your group, whether they are clients or research subjects. I have found this to be particularly appropriate if I'm working on a branding assignment or one in which we need to generate names or solicit feedback to names and positioning. It's also a great way to help people remember each other's names, or for a group that already knows each other to learn something new about their colleagues.

The exercise is based on the premise that every name has a story behind it. And if you give people a minute to tell their name story, you set the tone for what will be a warm, personal conversation.

Do you have a family name, an invented name, a nickname, a name that you love, or a name that you wish your parents had never given you, a name that is hard to pronounce or an unexpected name? In some cultures names denote social standing, or special qualities, skills, or powers. Among some people, knowing a person's "true name" can be used for blessing or curse.

Like Johnny Cash's "A Boy Named Sue," names can have a powerful influence on the course of our lives.

Ice Breaker

~10 minutes

Easy

Set Up Time:	30 seconds
Sharing:	less than 1 minute per person
Team Size:	individuals or groups of any size
Materials Needed:	none

Tip

As facilitator, start this off with your own story, which will help to set the tone and clarify expectations.

How to Do It

Keep it simple:

As we go around the room, please tell us your name, or nickname, and tell us the "story" behind your name. For example, is your name one that has been carried through generations, a name you like, a name from marriage? Who gave you your name? How do you feel about your name?

Your Experiments and Notes

Memoir Nuggets

Ice Breaker

~7 minutes

Easy

I recently worked with a client to understand how wearing a certain type of contact lens impacts lifestyle. My research design incorporated several stages of work and more storytelling than rapid-fire Q&A. I wanted to set the stage for the work with an interesting intro exercise and decided it might be fun to ask my Gen X and Gen Y research participants to imagine that they had just written a memoir and tell us what the title would be. The approach was delightful, and revealed much about the participants' attitudes.

Set Up Time:	1 minute
Sharing:	less than 1 minute per person
Team Size:	individuals or groups of any size
Materials Needed:	none

How to Do It

I'd like to start off with a fun way to introduce ourselves. I'd like you to imagine that you have just completed a memoir of your life thus far. What would you call it? As we go around the room tell us the title and a little behind it. I don't want you to think of this as a big, scary exercise, so I'll take the plunge first. I'd probably call my book, *Hangin' in the Kitchen with Laurie* because I love to cook and my kitchen seems to be the special place where my family and friends gather, we tell stories, have fun, and eat delicious food.

Your Experiments and Notes

Tip

It's very important for you to be the first model and offer an example that conveys the type of information that you are looking for in a limited amount of time. You don't want to hear a life story at this time, just a little headline nugget.

Talk Show Guest

You can use this quick introductory exercise with client teams or consumer teams. In addition to being a great Ice Breaker, it's a delightful way to inform a group of your expertise, or share something aside from professional credentials in which you feel accomplished.

Set Up Time:	1 minute
Run Time:	2 minutes
Sharing:	less than 1 minute per person
Team Size:	groups of any size
Materials Needed:	none

How to Do It

I'd like to start off with a fun way to introduce ourselves. I'd like you to imagine that you have just been invited to be a guest on your favorite talk show. As we go around the room tell us what special talent or skill has brought you here today. I'll start off so you'll get what I mean.

I'm here because I make a really great pot of soup. I know how to find the best ingredients, put them together, and stir them up so that they make an exquisite, healthy, hearty meal. That's my special talent.

Now this example, which I've used many times, is true and it's also a metaphor for the way I work with teams. By presenting my introduction in this manner, I've set the stage that this will not be the typical boring laundry list of accomplishments but something that is more memorable and personal.

Your Experiments and Notes

_____

_____

_____

_____

_____

_____

_____

Tip

As with other exercises, it's very important for you to be the first model and offer an example that conveys the type of information that you are looking for in a limited amount of time. There's a bit of a balancing act here. A little bragging is fine, but you don't want to present yourself in a way that is so lofty that everyone else will feel inferior.

Magical Gift

This is a delightful little exercise that you can use to set a friendly, creative tone whether with clients or research participants. The idea is for each member of the team to give a "gift" to another member of the team. The gift can be a real object in the room, or something in someone's possession, or it can be something that you draw and give to someone else. The giver bestows a "magical" or special power on the object. (Assure people that they'll get their item back at the end of the meeting, if it's something that belongs to them.) While the exercise works well as a first encounter, it can be even more effective to use on the morning of your second workday if you are conducting a multi-day session. Then the "gifts" can be tailored to the personalities of those present.

Ice Breaker
6+ minutes
Easy

Set Up Time:	1 minute
Run Time:	2 minutes
Sharing:	30 seconds per person
Team Size:	groups of any size as long as you have the time
Materials Needed:	imagination

How to Do It

We are about to begin an important meeting and I would like us to go around the room and give each other a gift that will be useful as we work together. I'm going to model this first. (*Speaking, for example, to the person on my right*) I'm going to give you this purple marker; it's not just any marker, but a special one. Purple is my favorite color, and when you use this marker your comments and ideas will be very exciting, and lead to a real breakthrough."

Another example:

I'm drawing a crystal ball on this sticky note and I'm going to give it to you, and you will find that the crystal ball gives you fantastic vision into the future.

The exercise is complete when everyone has received a gift.

Your Experiments and Notes

Tip

You will want to adapt your opening line to the situation, for example, the commencement of a meeting, or second day, and the type of work you will be doing together, whether research or idea generation.

Who's Your Muse?

This is a fun way to add spice to meeting introductions. Ask participants to tell you who inspires them; who encourages them to go beyond, to experiment, to take risks. This very simple exercise can have a powerful impact on your discussion. You can glean insights into values and cultural motifs, bring some humor into the meeting from the start, and inspire different kinds of thinking and problem solving.

Ice Breaker

~6 minutes

Easy

Set Up Time:	under 1 minute
Run Time:	2 minutes
Sharing:	30 seconds to 1 minute per person
Team Size:	groups of any size
Materials Needed:	none

How to Do It

Here are some different ways to frame the question:

Who is your Muse? Is there someone in your life, a real person or a character, someone you know directly or someone you have heard or read about who inspires you? As we go around the room introducing ourselves, introduce your Muse as well, and let's invite our Muses' thinking into this room as we work together.

Or . . .

If you could invite anyone into this meeting today, real or imaginary, someone you know or perhaps someone you have just heard or read about whose expertise or approach to thinking you would love to tap into today, who would that be? As we go around the room, introduce yourself and this other person. And imagine through the day that your Muse is sitting on your shoulder and can offer you encouragement, advice, wisdom, insights, whatever you need as we work together.

Or . . .

You can also substitute language of hero/heroine or great inventor, or an historical figure who you admire, or an artist, or literary character, etc.

Your Experiments and Notes

Tips

As facilitator or moderator, model the exercise by giving an example of your own, and present this with the type of brevity that you are looking for from your participants.

Take notes of the names or types of people that your participants mention, because it can be quite helpful in referring back to them in later discussion or exercises.

Bread-Breaking Ceremony

This is a wonderful exercise to launch an important project, to bring a new team together, or to revitalize a long-standing team. It's better for working with client teams than for qualitative research.

It's my adaptation of the many welcoming ceremonies I participated in when traveling through the former Soviet Union with a musical diplomacy group. We would enter a small town and be greeted by a local chorus who would invite us to "break bread" with them before singing together.

I first experimented with this exercise in a business setting about a dozen years ago, during a multi-phase assignment incorporating strategic visioning, consumer research, and product concept generation. In the initial strategic phase, two client teams, with very different cultures, were coming together to explore the possibility of developing a new business venture. I wanted to lay the groundwork for them to start a new culture together, and to get to know each other in a warm, inviting way. This was our Ice Breaker exercise and it proved to be a powerful yeast to our creative collaboration.

Ice Breaker, Teambuilding

7+ minutes

Easy, but requires planning

Set Up Time:	2 minutes
Run Time:	5+ minutes, depending upon how large a team
Sharing:	allow 30 seconds to a minute per person
Team Size:	from small to large groups
Materials Needed:	a large, round, unsliced loaf of bread, preferably an artisanal or handmade bakery item, wrapped in a nice napkin and placed on a plate; a small bowl of course-ground kosher or sea salt

How to Do It

Guideline to explain this to your group—

We are going to be working together on an exciting venture, and many of you are new to each other. Let's begin with a bread breaking ceremony. It's an old custom; perhaps you are familiar with this from your family. Pull off a piece of bread, dip it into the salt, and then pass the bread and salt onto the next person. As you pass the bread and salt along please introduce yourself to the team and offer a wish for how we will work together, and then of course, enjoy the bread!

Tip

This takes a bit of planning to purchase your ingredients ahead of time and keep the bread fresh.

Your Experiments and Notes

Imaginary Dish

You'll probably notice some running themes in this book. Music and food often sneak into my professional world. This exercise is one that will be easier to do if you happen to enjoy and feel comfortable around food. It's fun, but unpredictable, though every time I've used it in a session with clients, or as an opener for a large presentation for research colleagues, it has been successful. It can be particularly exciting when you have a large group of people coming together from different geographies.

Ice Breaker

Homework Assignment

~15 minutes in session

Moderate

Set Up Time:	Include this as a pre-session homework assignment for participants to bring in items from home or elsewhere.
Run Time:	15+ minutes
Sharing:	30 seconds to 1 minute per person
Team Size:	groups of any size as long as you have the time
Materials Needed:	a variety of food ingredients from participants with an example of your own, preferably items that can be transported without difficulty and can be left at room temperature for at least a day

How to Do It

Include something like the following in your pre-session invitation—

Please bring a small amount of a food ingredient with you that you particularly enjoy eating and that is representative of your _____ (*locale, your family traditions, however you want to frame the exercise*). This should be something that you can easily transport to our meeting and that can remain at room temperature for a day. It can be something that you typically eat raw or cooked—we won't be cooking here, and we may not actually eat it.

In Session

Use this as part of your introductions or early in your work together. Invite participants to show the foods or ingredients they brought, and say a little bit about the food and why they chose it. Then in a quick, collaborative brainstorm (don't bother writing down the ideas) ask people to speculate how we might use all or many of the ingredients that people brought to create one or more different food dishes. Add your own ideas to the mix,

Tip

As moderator, bring one or two ingredients of your own with you that you can use in your introduction.

and if you are a foodie you just might inspire your team with unique and tasty combinations.

Chances are you will learn a lot about who your team members are and how they will work together. You can use this as a jumping off place to talk about components of innovation and creativity—e.g., spontaneity, flexibility, open-mindedness, collaboration, combining "ingredients" in unexpected ways, and more.

Please see *Kitchen Magic* (page 94) for another way to use diverse ingredients for connection making.

Your Experiments and Notes

Additional Ice Breaker Experiments and Observations

TRUTHSAYERS

I use the term "Truthsayers" for this section, with a nod to Frank Herbert's science fiction novel *Dune*. In that world, a Truthsayer is one who could detect truth when it is being told.

Neuroscientists argue that the best way to get insights into human emotions is by having subjects hooked up to sensors that monitor brain waves, eye movement or skin response. Behavioral economists suggest that we can't get accurate insights into decision-making by asking the traditional "Why?" question, because consumers don't generally make rational decisions.[1] Rather, they make decisions based on emotions, which they may not be aware of. Consumers make choices from what is available at the time, even if those choices contradict their earlier decision-making criteria. When asked about their choices, they try to express themselves rationally, in order to justify or explain their behavior. It is often the rationalizations that researchers hear in focus groups; partly because of the way we frame our questions.

I'm not an expert in neuroscience or behavioral economics, but I know from more than two decades' experience conducting innovation sessions and qualitative research that we can get honest answers and robust insights from participants if we create the right environment and use the right questions and exercises. Our goal is to help participants access their experiences and emotions.

Activities to help research participants recall behaviors and experiences, and get in touch with, and talk about, emotions

Creating the right environment

One of the challenges with traditional focus groups is that we bring strangers into an uncomfortable, often quite sterile environment, sit them around an imposing boardroom-type table and then prod them with lots of questions. And to add to the discomfort, they know they are being watched from behind

1. Wendy Gordon. "How Behavioral Economics is Challenging the Very Essence of Qualitative Research," QRCA VIEWS, Spring 2011.

the mirror. That's why I try, whenever feasible, to arrange for a living-room style setting with couches, chairs, and low tables. And even when we have no choice but to work in a boardroom-style venue, we can still encourage a group of individuals to get to know each other and work together in a more comfortable atmosphere that feels like a group of friends rather than strangers.

Key among the tools at our disposal for creating a comfortable atmosphere are interpersonal skills of warmth and energy in welcoming participants, in genuine listening, and in using words and tone of voice that say: "This will be a pleasant experience; we'll have fun; we'll learn more about ourselves and each other." Fellow QRCA member Ricardo Lopez calls this "moderating with spirit." Since comfort level and feelings of attraction occur in the first few minutes of meeting people, part of creating the right environment includes using an ice breaker or warm-up introductory exercise; many of these are in the first section of this book.

Using questions and exercises to elicit stories

Once you have set the right tone you can then move on to the heart of the discussion. Your client may have suggested "100" questions to ask the participants; my goal is always to find ways to design research to minimize the Q&A game and maximize the storytelling. Stories, according to Bob Dickman, are "facts wrapped in emotions."[2]

2. Richard Maxwell and Robert Dickman. *The Elements of Persuasion: Use Storytelling to Pitch Better, Sell Faster & Win More Business.* HarperBusiness, 2007.

Stories generally suggest answers to many questions in ways that are more engaging for participants, and yield more insights for our clients. We get beyond the *why* and hear the *how, what, when,* and *where.* We engage in conversation, rather than inquisition, and we use exercises to help participants recall behaviors and experiences, get in touch with their emotions, and feel more comfortable sharing them in a group.

When people are comfortable and relaxed, they are more likely to open up. By using storytelling and creative exercises we engage the whole brain. We make it clear that there are no "wrong" answers; we want to hear our participants' perceptions, beliefs, and ideas. The result is that we do elicit those candid and rich responses.

Some of the exercises in this section are ethnographic in nature. We can't always have the ability to get into people's homes and other environments to observe how they live, work, and play. However, by bringing into the group pictures or videos or collages we can get closer to that experience. Often "truth" is revealed in dramatic ways. I'm reminded of projects in the organic personal care arena, where our participants told us that they primarily buy and use the finest natural and organic hair care and skin care items. However, the photographs they showed us of their personal care closets contained far more products that were filled with synthetic ingredients, than those with natural or organic ingredients. Seeing the pictures enabled us to learn more and focus the discussion in deeper ways to understand why they think of themselves as natural or organic shoppers, but behave differently.

Visual exercises can sometimes communicate deeper truths than words. For example, creating symbols and simple drawings can be powerful revelatory tools. In working with people who have type 2 diabetes, we asked them to draw a symbol representing how they first felt when they heard their diabetes diagnosis. Years later their drawings and stories have stayed with me: the woman who depicted the Hangman, the young man who drew the Grim Reaper. Could they have expressed those powerful feelings in words first? I don't know. But creating the symbols helped them talk about their feelings in very honest and powerful ways.

I hope you will look through the array of Truthsayer exercises here, and find a few that you feel comfortable experimenting with. Adapt them; make them your own. It may be that by weaving in just one Truthsayer exercise within a group discussion, you will get richer insights from the other 99 questions as well.

Snapshot or "FlipVid"

This exercise is designed to quickly gather images and concrete details of certain aspects in the lives of research participants. You ask them to imagine that they've just captured a situation in either a snapshot or as a brief video clip.

I've used this in countless research assignments whose aim was new product or positioning ideas. For example, in qualitative groups on breakfast foods, I asked participants to give us a snapshot or quick video of what was going on in the kitchen during a typical weekday morning. While it's not a substitute for being in their kitchen, it does provide valuable insights.

Another application for the exercise is for initial introductions in a group or one-on-one setting.

Set Up Time:	1 minute
Run Time:	5+ minutes
Sharing:	30 seconds to 1 minute per person
Team Size:	you can do this with individuals or groups of any size as long as you have the time
Materials Needed:	just memory and imagination

How to Do It

Your positioning will vary depending up your task. Here's a sample script:

I'd like you to imagine that I had a video camera with me and I was at your side as you came home from work on a typical day last week. What would I have seen as you opened the door? What did you do first? Who or what greeted you? What were the sounds, smells, emotions? Show us that scene, in as much vivid detail as you can.

Your Experiments and Notes

Truthsayer, Ice Breaker

5+ minutes

Easy

Tips

The details of the stories are important. You will understand your participants better and you will likely find yourself coming back and revisiting some of the themes or elements of their descriptions later on in your research discussion. You may have to tease out the details by asking them to tell you more.

As If an Alien

Ethnographic researchers work hard to cast their own assumptions aside as they try to understand deeply what is going on in the life and activities of another human being. No detail is too small; every behavior is new, and fascinating. This simple exercise invites the researcher and research subject to view the world through a fresh set of lenses, which is why I call it "as if an alien." I'll explain a bit further.

If I ask typical Americans to tell me about their cold symptoms, or what it's like not to get a good night's sleep, or what they feel like when they get a belly ache from overeating, I can pretty much predict the key words, phrases, and descriptions that will be used in their responses. But if I ask typical Americans to describe their experiences and imagine that I am an alien from another planet, and I have no idea what a cold is, or what sleep is, or what a stomach ache is, then the research subjects have to work a bit harder to communicate meaning. They have to get creative, perhaps use analogy or metaphor or something else that this "alien" just might be able to understand. I think you can imagine how robust and insight producing this exercise can be.

Truthsayer

12–15 minutes

Easy

Tip

Give participants a few minutes to collect their thoughts and then have volunteers talk. Keep probing as much as you can.

Set Up Time:	1 minute
Run Time:	3+ minutes
Sharing:	2 to 3 minutes per person
Team Size:	individuals, groups of any size
Materials Needed:	paper and pen or pencil for each participant

How to Do It

I'd like you to imagine for the next few minutes that I have recently arrived on planet Earth and am trying to understand what you human beings are all about. Can you please try to educate me about what it's like when you _____ (fill in the blank relative to the task, e.g., have a cold?). I see these ads where humans seem to be unhappy about something called "a cold." Have you ever had a cold? Please teach me, tell me what that is like for you. If you want to use pictures as well as words that is good, too. Sometimes we aliens understand pictures better.

Your Experiments and Notes

Show & Tell

When I was in grade school I loved our weekly show-and-tell sessions where we would select something of interest, perhaps a beautiful fallen leaf or a rock or a book or toy, and we would show it to schoolmates and tell why it mattered to us. In similar fashion, using a little show-and-tell exercise in a research setting can be engaging and insightful.

Truthsayer

Homework assignment

5+ minutes in session

Easy

Set Up Time:	send your instructions to do the exercise as part of the research invitation
Sharing:	under 1 minute per person
Team Size:	you can do this with individuals or groups of any size as long as you have the time
Materials Needed:	participants bring

How to Do It

In an ongoing series of studies for a vitamin/supplements manufacturer, I asked research participants to:

> Bring in something that you consider your "secret weapon" to keep you healthy. If you can't literally bring in the item, bring a photograph or a simple sketch and be prepared to talk about it.

In this series of groups, I sometimes used the exercise at the beginning as part of the introductions, and other times left it until a bit later. While we would see some things we expected, a lot of participants brought in their favorite multi-vitamins, for example, we would also see things that were more esoteric: home remedies or local brews and a slew of other items that greatly broadened our perspectives. I recall a woman who brought a picture of her dog; she described that since she had the dog she lost a tremendous amount of weight because she was committed to giving the dog long walks daily, something she had never done before. Another woman brought in a picture of her spouse, who is her partner in leading a healthy lifestyle and cheers her on and supports her efforts to eat right and exercise.

In a series of projects for a natural and organic personal care manufacturer, I've frequently asked participants to bring in photographs of their personal care products closets or shelves, "wherever you store items like shampoos and skin care products." It's fascinating how differently our research subjects interpreted "natural and organic" compared to our clients' interpretations. As we would go around the room in the *Show & Tell*, we would see photograph after photograph from people who said that they were committed to using only the finest products and were careful label readers, yet in a closet of 20 items, there would be only one or two products that my client considered natural or organic.

While simple to implement, *Show & Tell* can prove to be quite revealing of consumer behaviors and attitudes.

Your Experiments and Notes

Fantastic Voyage

For a consumer ideation session to create improvements in a line of products for indigestion I designed this exercise to flush out new language and imagery. You can apply this sensory imagination approach to any "ingestible," whether food or medicine, and vary specific directions as appropriate to your topic.

Truthsayer, Connection-Maker

12–15 minutes

Easy

Set Up Time:	2 minutes
Run Time:	5 minutes
Sharing:	about 1 minute per person
Team Size:	small to medium-sized groups
Materials Needed:	paper and pen or pencil for each participant

How to Do It

We're going to start with a little relaxation, a few quiet, slow breaths to get us in the mood for a *Fantastic Voyage*. Perhaps some of you heard of that science fiction movie where a group of doctors and scientists are miniaturized to the size of atoms and go inside a person's body to make repairs. Well for this exercise, I'd like you to imagine that you are inside your own body and different parts are having a conversation with each other about your heartburn. What is your mouth telling your tummy? What is going on with your tongue, your teeth, and your esophagus? What are they feeling? Saying? Jot some notes down and then we will talk about it.

Give participants three to five minutes to get into the exercise and write notes. You can then ask them to reveal their inner conversations and use the whole team to make connections and generate ideas, or you can instruct individuals to use their body memories to create ideas that relate to or that address your task.

Your Experiments and Notes

"Dear John" Letter

I was inspired to try this exercise by a conversation with a restaurant client and it proved to be a great success. We were working on a project trying to understand brand loyalty in this category. We know that there is a lot of switching back and forth from one dining chain to another, but our research participants were supposedly pretty loyal to our client. What we learned was sobering. It was far easier for participants to write a "Dear John" break up letter to our client's brand than to the other major competitors. (So much for "loyalty!")

I've used this many times since and found it quite revealing and effective for getting at brand or product or service perceptions, and identifying opportunities for improvement.

Truthsayer

12–15 minutes

Easy

Set Up Time:	2 minutes
Run Time:	5+ minutes
Sharing:	1 minute per person
Team Size:	individuals, or groups of any size as long as you have the time
Materials Needed:	paper and pen or pencil for each participant

How to Do It

A "Dear John" letter is a break-up letter. Did you ever write one of those to a boyfriend or girlfriend? Or were you ever on the receiving end?

Well, for the next few minutes, I'd like you to put yourself in the role of someone who is ending a relationship with a formerly favorite _____ (*restaurant, or brand, or product that you are working on*). Write a note to explain why the relationship is over. And tell them who is likely to replace them in your heart, attention, and pocketbook.

Tip

Give participants a good 5 minutes to write the letter, observing how they are working, in case you can speed up or need to add a little more time. Then ask for volunteers to read their letters aloud to the group. If you don't hear all the letters, be sure to read them afterwards.

Your Experiments and Notes

_____

_____

_____

_____

_____

_____

Collage 101

Asking research participants to create a collage—an arrangement of pictures and words pasted on a large sheet of paper—has become commonplace in qualitative research. This wasn't always the case. The objective behind a collage is to help participants articulate some "truths" about their lives, or attitudes, or perceptions about a brand or a product category. Collage can still have an important place in a researcher's tool chest. There are even new digital tools to help participants create collages. These may result in more beautiful collages, although not necessarily richer insights.

In a research setting I prefer to give collages as a homework assignment rather than during the session itself, so that participants can take time with them. A collage can be an intriguing window into a person's home, family life, or what they really keep stocked in the breakfast pantry. While it's not a substitute for an in-home visit, it can be very useful. A key to success is to give specific directions for making their collages and provide questions or areas that you would like participants to respond to in their creations.

How you use the collages will vary. You will get the most mileage by allowing enough time to show and tell about the works and probe beyond what is presented.

Truthsayer, Ice Breaker

Homework assignment

~10+ minutes discussion in session

+15 minutes if making collages in session

Easy

Set Up Time:	include in a pre-group homework assignment so that participants may take as long with the activity as they like; be specific in what you want them to create
Sharing:	1 minute or more per person
Materials Needed:	none if this is a homework assignment

How to Do It

A few ideas to consider:

- Use collage showing as part of the initial warm-up phase of a group.

- After a person has presented her work, ask her to sum up what she has shown in a brief title.

- If you have a large team and little time, ask participants to focus on one particular nugget of their work that they found interesting or surprising as they were creating it.

- After showing the collages, ask research participants what they saw as the "big themes" or areas where many people were in agreement or disagreement.

- A final tip, take photographs of the collages and include some, if not all, in the final report or presentation.

As an in-session assignment, allow at least 15 minutes for participants to create their collages, plus time for show and tell. Have an array of materials on hand including scissors, magazines, photographs or other images, tape or glue, and heavy paper for mounting.

Your Experiments and Notes

Color Wheel

Color inspires, and entwines with emotion, memory and meaning. So of course, it makes good sense for researchers and facilitators to have a number of color-related exercises in their tool boxes! Here are a few of my favorites: Gut-Level Voting or reactions to concept, prototype or other creative stimulus; Personal Mood Indicator; and Summary of an Experience.

Truthsayer

3–10 minutes

Easy

Set Up Time:	1 minute
Run Time:	varies depending on exercise; these can be done quickly, under 10 minutes for a team of about 5–12 participants
Sharing:	about 1 minute per person
Team Size:	individuals, groups of any size
Materials Needed:	color stimuli of your choosing, e.g., a variety of colored markers, a big box of colored crayons or pencils, color chips from a paint store, Pantone color chips, colored sticky dots

How to Do These

Gut Level Voting

*Give participants (up to 3) color swatches, cards, dots or stickies, e.g., green for **Go** or **I Like It**; red for **Stop** or **Don't Like It**; and white or another color for **Neutral**, or **On the Fence**. Have participants vote with color in response to viewing a concept, prototype, or other creative stimuli. Then have them discuss their votes in more detail so that you hear their rationale.*

Personal Mood Indicator

Ask participants to quickly get in touch with how they are feeling about a topic or category or situation, by selecting from a wide variety of color options (from among markers, crayons, or swatches). Go around the group asking each person to show their true colors and discuss the meanings and emotions behind their selection.

Summary of an Experience

I love to do this to get an initial read on the way clients have viewed a research event like a focus group. We don't even have to use color stimuli, but rely on the language of color. My instructions:

What color best describes this _____ (*group, team*)? Give us the color and then the explanation behind it.

It's very important to get the rationale, because people assign different meanings to colors. For example: "Red, because this group was 'smokin' hot' with their passion for the topic and their ideas." Or, "Red, because they've clearly given us the message that we should put the brake on these ideas; they just didn't like them!"

Your Experiments and Notes

Scrapbook

I noticed a few years ago that when I assigned consumer teams a collage homework exercise, occasionally someone would walk into the group with something much more elaborate than a single sheet of paper with pictures and words. Scrapbooking was coming into vogue and many people liked the excuse to show off their creative talents. I hesitated to ask participants to spend the additional time to create a scrapbook until I had a project where I thought it would help our research objectives and we could build in enough time to let participants talk through their creations. The opportunity presented itself when we designed a complex "Shoppers Immersion" in which we coached our client team members to be researchers, and to work shoulder-to-shoulder with the shoppers. We wanted to give our clients a way to get rich insights into our research participants' lives, and into their experience shopping for certain food categories at specific stores. We felt that the scrapbooks would make it easier to facilitate conversations between client/researchers and shoppers. The approach worked remarkably well and I've since used this on several other assignments.

Truthsayer

Homework assignment

12–20+ minutes in session

Easy

Set Up Time:	assign as a pre-session "homework" activity, but allow a minute or two during the session to tell research participants how you want to review their scrapbooks in the session
Sharing:	2 to 20 minutes per person; time will vary depending upon your research design
Team Size:	individuals, groups of any size
Materials Needed:	none

How to Do It

Write out the details of your scrapbook homework assignment and have your recruiters read it to participants before they agree to participate in your study. Then make sure the recruiters mail or email the assignment and follow up to see that it has been understood and completed.

Be specific about what you want to see in the scrapbook. Here is an example:

Tips

If you are going to ask participants to do all this work ahead of time you want to make sure that you have enough time to review their creations in detail.

At the end of your research be sure you collect the scrapbooks and review them closely as you analyze the results of your study.

Please create a "scrapbook" (*6 or more pages*) that illustrates and brings to life yourself and others who share your household. Include pictures and jot a few words that tell us about who you are, and what's really important to you. Please respond to each of the following areas:

1. Introduce us to your home and family with pictures and a few words.

2. Introduce us to what daily life is like for you with pictures and a few words.

3. What do you like to do for fun? Show us with pictures and a few words.

4. What makes everyday life a challenge? Show us with pictures and a few words.

5. Tell us your story about _____ (*product, service, category, or brand*) with pictures and a few words.

6. What does this _____ (*product, service, category, or brand*) mean for you in your life?

Occasionally a participant will create something filled with family photos and they just don't want to leave the scrapbook, or they want to remove the family photos from it. You might want to take digital photos of the scrapbooks as back up.

Final Tip

For confidentiality purposes, ask participants to only show first names in photo identification.

Electronic Variation

If you're doing online rather than face-to-face research, this activity can be done using any one of a variety of online research platforms in which participants would create and upload their scrapbooks electronically.

Your Experiments and Notes

A Day in the Life

This exercise is powerful when you are working with a client team and you want to bring the "voice" of the customer or consumer into the mix in a dynamic, empathetic way.

Truthsayer, Connection-Maker

-20 minutes

Moderate

Set Up Time:	2 minutes
Run Time:	5+ minutes
Sharing:	1 minute per person
Team Size:	small to medium-size teams, about 6–15 people
Materials Needed:	paper and pen or pencil for each participant

How to Do It

Write thumbnail sketches ahead of time of the types of people who might be users of your client's products or services.

I do this on individual sticky notes or index cards. I base the characters on whatever real demographic and lifestyle information I may have, but try to stretch the boundaries a bit. Often my invented personas are based on real people I have encountered in my life.

Here are some examples:

Amy is 36, mom of twin teens, lives in Peoria, sells Mary Kay cosmetics and loves to kick box.

John, retired from the world of finance, is a 65 year-old blogger who writes about wine. He lives in a loft in New York with his two black Labs, plays the violin, and loves to travel.

Suzie, 47, a recently divorced mom with three kids, is currently driving a cab in Chicago and trying to get back into her real work which is broadcasting.

Here's how I position the exercise:

Let's bring some potential (*consumers/customers*) into our session. I'm going to hand out a brief thumbnail sketch that I wrote out ahead of time. You might be given a role that is close to who you are or someone who is quite different! The idea is for you to imagine a day-in-the-life of this person. Write some notes. Where does the person live? With whom? What do they have for breakfast? For dinner? What's hard for them? What's fun?

Use questions or prompts that will be most relevant for your topic.

> I'm going to give you about 3 minutes to create this day-in-the-life scenario and then we'll share it and see what new ideas this might suggest.

You can debrief the exercise by having each person talk about their character and then collecting themes and ideas as a full group. Or you can have participants pair up and talk among themselves, first sharing each individual's work, and then collaborating together to create beginning connections and ideas. Then you would capture those pair-team ideas in a full group discussion. The latter is a safer bet if you have some participants who are less inventive. However you field the final output, encourage participants to talk about the ideas that emerged, more than the details of the life stories, in order to keep the time manageable.

Your Experiments and Notes

Inspiration from Archetypes

Plato referred to Archetypes as ideal templates or "forms." Carl Jung spoke of them as images from the collective unconscious. Heady concepts, for sure, and there are myriad ways a market researcher or innovation consultant might use Archetypes in facilitating learning, gathering insights or ideas.

Truthsayer, Connection-Maker

15–30 minutes

Moderate

A few years ago I came across a stunning collection of Archetype cards produced by Carolyn Myss (*www.myss.com*). I've had great success in using them in client and research sessions. For example, in working with a client in the health services arena that was looking for a new way to communicate its message to physicians and patients, I was impressed by the depth of thinking and ideas that the cards and the exercise provoked.

There are a variety of Archetype cards you can purchase. Myss' version contains the name of the Archetype (e.g., Mother, Judge, Warrior, Trickster); with a description of its *light attribute* (e.g., Trickster: "transcending convention, stuffiness, and predictable behavior") and its *shadow attribute* (e.g., Trickster: "manipulating others through duplicity"). And there's a lovely illustration to go with the words.

Set Up Time:	2–3 minutes
Run Time:	about 10 minutes
Sharing:	1 minute per person
Team Size:	individuals, or groups of any size as long as you have the time
Materials Needed:	archetype cards (whether this version or something of your own creation); paper and pen or pencil for each participant

How to Do It

Philosophers, psychologists, cultural anthropologists, artists, marketers and others have been working with Archetypes for years. Whether you know anything in particular about them is not necessary for this exercise to be valuable. We'll use this as poetry or art and see where it leads. I'll just ask you to approach this with an open mind. I've spread out a number of cards on the table and each has the name of an Archetype and a description of the light and dark aspect of each. I want you to just come up to the table and select three to five of these cards that somehow "call out" to you as you think about our task (*e.g., to create a new communications strategy, or a new positioning, or way to talk about brand benefits, etc.).* Bring the cards back to your seat and read through them, let them sink into your mind. Perhaps one card seems most intriguing. Reflect on what the card says and see how you might tie it back to our challenge today. Jot down some notes.

Give participants 5 minutes to do this, then have them get into pair teams.

Now I'd like you to show your cards to your team mate and see where the cards might take you in terms of a story and some beginning ideas for our task.

Give teams 5 minutes or so to do this and then collect their stories, connections or ideas. If your participants offer intriguing stories but nothing "concrete" in terms of themes or ideas, you can gently push them further for "second generation ideas" having them work in their pair teams first.

Your Experiments and Notes

Improvs

Improvisation is a fantastic way to bring new ideas to light. You can use
this technique in a wide range of situations with client teams or consumer
research participants. There are always a few "hams" in any group; if you are
going to try this out, get volunteers to be the first ones up to do an improv
exercise. Generally what happens is that most other members of the group
see the fun and feel more empowered to volunteer for the next improv.

    I use improvs in a variety of ways. When working with a client team, it
is generally to bring a voice of the consumer or customer into our thought
process, for example:

**Truthsayer,
Connection-
Maker**

15–30+ minutes

Moderate

- On an assignment to create a portfolio of new frozen novelties for
  a client team we set up a series of improvs. One featured the client
  team leader as a soccer mom shuttling her three kids in the van on
  a hot summer day.

- In an assignment on children's allergy relief products, we set up various scenes of parents and kids in the playground and at a bus stop.

When working with research participants, improvs are more often used
to get deeper insights about their feelings toward a category, brand, product,
or idea. For example, for a hair care manufacturer, we set a scene at a dance
and asked consumers to act out how they felt after using a new shampoo. In
another project, we created a variety of situations and consumers did improvisations using new mobile phone services.

Basic Rules and Reminders of Improv

- Improv is small group storytelling
- Improvs contain a series of *offers*, e.g., any action or dialog that
  advances a scene. Always *accept* the offer of a partner in the scene.
  Say "yes and"—accept, and then add to your partner's statement or
  action; don't negate other people
- Avoid asking lots of questions
- Establish a location
- Be specific, provide details
- You don't have to be funny

- Tell a story with your actions; do something whenever you can instead of just talking about it

- We want to see true aspects within the story

Set Up Time:	5 minutes to clear a space for the "stage," explain the rules, give the first situation (which you may have thought up ahead of time)
Run Time:	10–15+ minutes
Sharing:	debrief and capture connections and ideas for as long as time permits and the exercise yields fruitful results
Team Size:	generally more workable with a maximum total group size of 15, and improv performer teams of two to four
Materials Needed:	a meeting space with a clear floor area for two to four people to move around comfortably

Tip

I will write out a simple situation on an index card or just whisper it to the improv players. For the examples noted at left, my instructions were: "mom and kids in a car on hot summer day;" "mom and friend on a bench in playground;" and "two adults at a dance."

How to Do It

We're going to bring _____ (this task, these ideas, etc.) to life with a fun exercise which we call an improv or improvisational theater. Anyone ever participate in something like this before? Good, we'll ask you to be the first volunteers! I'm going to clear a little space for our "stage."

I generally push chairs out of the way and mark off a space on the floor with masking tape.

Now I'm going to call on _____ volunteers (2 to 4, depending upon how many you want for your first scene). I'm going to give you a few words to set the scene, then give you and your fellow actors one minute (not longer!) to make any other decisions you want about the scene and then will call "go." I'll let you run the improv for a couple of minutes until it naturally ends or I call "stop." While the improv is taking place before us, I would like everyone to pay close attention. Afterwards we are going to collect your observations and ideas that were inspired by the activity.

Huddle with the improv performers and explain the scenario for the improv that you have written up ahead of time. Don't let observers hear the setup.

I will usually run this exercise long enough so that at least 3 teams get a chance to do an improv, with each improv lasting no more than 3 minutes.

Sometimes, an improv just doesn't work. Don't get distressed. Don't embarrass anyone. Just acknowledge that sometimes an improv falls flat. See if another team would like to get up and have a try at it, and give them a different situation. In spite of an occasional failure this exercise is a great one for your toolkit. A playground role-play paid off for a client marketing children's allergy relief with a new single dose, on-the-go package.

Your Experiments and Notes

BodyMap

My colleague Reva and I were working on a multi-phase new products assignment for a confectionery client, exploring the role of mint and mint combined with chocolate. One phase of qualitative groups was held in Seattle, a place with extremely high mint consumption at the time. We used this exercise to get beyond the typical responses we were hearing to our questions of what people like about mint, and this approach generated many insights. I've since used this numerous times, primarily within a qualitative research setting.

Truthsayer, Connection-Maker

10 minutes

Moderate

Set Up Time:	2 minutes
Run Time:	5 minutes
Sharing:	30 seconds to 1 minute per team
Team Size:	groups of 6–12
Materials Needed:	flip-chart paper and markers spread out in a room

How to Do It

I find that it helps if you sketch out an outline of a human body ahead of time. This doesn't have to be fancy or artistic at all; a simple outline will suffice. Your directions to the team will vary based on your project objectives, but here's a sample script that you can use after you have revealed the BodyMap outlines.

For the next few minutes I'd like you and your partner to discuss what happens to you when you eat something with mint. What effect does it have on various aspects of your body or mind? Each team has a simple outline of a body. Please label the parts of the body that are affected including a few words that describe the affect that mint has on that part of the body. Don't worry about being technically precise in any way, a poetic approach is fine!

After participants have labeled their drawings ask them to present what they came up with and if necessary probe for more details. The result is likely to be interesting and surprising language about benefits, useful in product or positioning projects.

Your Experiments and Notes

Tip

Set up pair teams so that they can discuss ideas back and forth and feel less self-conscious about sharing what they have come up with.

Capturing Life in the Moment
(using video and audio diaries)

I was first exposed to the idea of asking research participants to create video or audio diaries through a collaborative project with Patricia Sunderland at Practica Group. Diaries can provide a fascinating insight-rich look into people's lives. While highly trained ethnographers can analyze diaries in depth, even a more general researcher can find great value in adding this approach to the Tool Box. A caution though is that this is a labor intense activity (days, not minutes) for the researcher to set up and analyze results, and it will demand one to two hours or more from research participants.

Recognizing the power of this activity, I've incorporated diaries in various research designs, including:

- after in-depth, in-home visits to understand how people clean their homes;

- with a select group of participants from an initial round of focus groups to capture how contact lens wearing fits into daily life activities. In a follow-up group we discussed the diary-keeping activity and what participants noticed about themselves and their routines.

Team Size:	relatively small groups—usually between 6 and 20 participants because of the labor and costs involved
Materials Needed:	hand-held video cameras or pocket-sized flip video cameras, small digital audio recorders, power cords or batteries for the recorders, equipment instruction sheets, detailed instructions to participants of what to capture in their diaries

How to Do It

In ethnographic research, no detail is too small. Your diary instructions should clearly outline what you expect your research subjects to show you or tell you about. I've usually set this up as a three-part assignment to take place over three to seven days. In Day 1, I ask the participant to introduce himself/herself and his or her environment. For the "middle days" I ask the participant to respond to specific questions about life activities, needs, usage, in relationship to the category/product/brands, etc. of our research topic. The final day is primarily for reflections on the diary keeping experience.

There are pros and cons to using video vs. audio diaries. In this age of YouTube and reality TV, video is a much more comfortable medium for participants to do than ever before, and of course, there are some aspects of behavior that can best be understood by seeing. Audio is excellent for more self-reflective situations and may be best for more sensitive topics.

After the diaries are complete and the equipment and diaries are returned, the researcher has the mighty task of reviewing, analyzing and likely selecting snippets to edit into a final presentation. My rule of thumb is that for every hour of diary, you as researcher will likely spend three hours or more on the back end. If you work with a professional video or audio editor, double the time for their work.

There are other ways to do this with a variety of online research platforms available. In some cases respondents are asked to keep relatively short diaries and they can upload their material directly to the platform for the researcher and others to view online.

Your Experiments and Notes

Additional Truthsayer Experiments and Observations

Energy Changers

A composer scores a piece contrasting moments of *pianissimo* (very soft) with *forté* (strong, loud). A cook plays with the heat of spices, the cooling creaminess of dairy, and temperatures from red hot to frozen. The choreographer incorporates dizzying twirls and then quiet stillness. These variations produce effects in the body, mind, and emotions.

The meeting convener also has a portfolio of options to play with for changing the energy of a group. Sound, music, movement, physical games, temperature (fresh air), food and beverages, and, of course, words can all be employed to achieve a particular impact on the discussion. I'm *not* suggesting a Machiavellian approach or manipulation, but I am suggesting that a good facilitator or researcher pays attention to the energy of the group discussion and is ready to effect change when it is required.

There are four key situations when energy or mood changing is called for:

The group is simply fatigued.

It can be physically and emotionally tiring to be a leader or participant in a discussion or idea session. As facilitator you want to raise the energy and help people feel refreshed so that they can be more productive. Having something to eat or drink, getting a little fresh air, just moving about and stretching, or playing vibrant music are all ways to revitalize flagging energy.

You want to help participants relax, so that they can reflect and call up memories of experiences.

Asking participants to sit quietly for a minute and pay attention to their breathing, playing soft music, and using your voice in a calm, quiet way can all contribute to setting the tone for such a reflective exercise.

Activities to fuel or recharge a group or to guide participants into quiet reflection

You want to create a playful distraction in order to fool the brain's self censor that hampers creativity.

Encouraging team members to get into a playful frame of mind, using toys and games, moving about the space, engaging in an activity that seemingly has no bearing on the task you are working, on helps participants to be relaxed and less vigilant about "being right" or "being smart." That's often when new ideas emerge. When we are not "working hard" to get ideas, when we relax that internal, critical self-judge who voices those Idea Killer phrases like "this won't work," or "it's too expensive," we're more likely to suggest ideas that are more novel and can then be developed further into something which is both new and implementable.

The group is off on a tangent and you want to get them back on track.

Employ a brief dramatic surge of music, aroma, visual stimuli, or a physical stretch to transition the team back on track.

When creating an Energy Changer, consider engaging multiple senses

Taste

If you are convening a group discussion or idea session of two hours or more, be sure to make arrangements to have some food and beverages available. If all of the choices are sugar-laden sweets, there is a good chance that your participants will react with a rush of energy and then a dramatic drop. I find that it is a good idea to have protein and whole foods like fruits, vegetables, nuts, cheese, and yogurt available to keep the blood sugar and energy level more constant. By the way, over the years I've had clients suggest that they would do a better job in a brainstorming session after dinner and drinks, particularly after beer or wine! I've never done a scientific study, but I can say definitively in my experience that a small amount of alcohol—a glass of beer or wine—relaxes some people so that they are more comfortable expressing themselves and letting their creativity emerge, but more consumption of alcohol seems to work against the process. Whenever I've been in a situation where innovation work has been scheduled after cocktails, when we look back later on the ideas generated, they are generally deemed of lesser quality.

Sound

There's an exercise in this chapter about using mood music in groups. But another simple thing you can do is to bring a single, small musical instrument to your meeting. I almost always travel with a set of brass Tibetan temple bells (much to the chagrin of airport TSA!). A light tap of the bells brings a stirring sound to the room that reverberates for almost a minute. The sound is beautiful, haunting, and an effective way to signal a change in direction. I often use the bells when convening a client team innovation session, as a reminder that we are entering a special place mentally in which we will proceed with our work. And I use them sparingly throughout the session to pull break-out teams together to rejoin the larger group. If you are not a fan of bells, you might experiment with a small hand drum or a rattle or shaker with a pleasing sound.

Aroma

Some years ago I worked with groups of consumers and natural healers on an aromatherapy assignment. I learned a few neat tips from them about using aroma to influence mood and energy. The healers used scented oils of botanicals and herbs like lavender, rose, and mint, heated on a diffuser, to help facilitate a quiet, reflective, meditative mood. And while I have done that on some occasions in session, I've found that a flame, even in a small, lit diffuser, can be a no-no in a conventional meeting room. A trick I learned from schoolteachers in the consumer group: an orange, cut open, or an orange pricked with cloves. These were aromatherapy favorites to help students stay alert when taking tests. Other participants in that project suggested a small bowl of coffee beans as olfactory stimulus.

Visual

Perusing beautiful or interesting pictures, whether as hardcopy handouts or in a two-minute slide show can be wonderful mental refreshment. My colleague Reva always carries an assortment of very intriguing, surrealistic pictures gleaned from magazines; she distributes them among a team when she wants to change the mood. The visuals can also be used to guide participants through a daydreaming or story-creation process leading to idea generation.

Physical Movement

I find it awfully difficult to sit still for more than an hour. Fanny fatigue sets
in. When I'm in my home office I have the luxury of being able to get up,
move about, snatch a breath of fresh air, refill the coffee cup or water glass,
and give the dog or cat a good "scrutching." Three minutes up and away from
my desk, doing physical things, is a great recharge for me. More often than
not, as I'm doing one of those things during my "break," I get another little
nugget of an idea or something related to what I'm working on. That's one
of the reasons why I am a firm proponent of getting participants up and out
of their seats every hour or so, even if just for a three-minute stretch.

Aside from the exercises listed in this chapter, there are many other ways
to introduce a quick physical recharge. For back room focus group listeners,
I encourage them to get up and walk the back room and closely focus in on
different participants in the group. They get a wider and deeper viewpoint
than they would by just by sitting in one spot.

In a group session where people know each other and physical touching
is culturally accepted, you can suggest a circle shoulder massage for a minute or two, then turn in the other direction and reciprocate the favor, and of
course be sure to thank your masseuse!

Fresh Air

In my experience, the absolute best venues to work in have windows that
let in fresh air, or a patio or outdoor area that you can use for a quick break
or brief activity. Even in less than perfect weather, a couple of minutes outside can be the best way to bring renewed vitality to a group discussion.
Unfortunately, conventional meeting rooms and focus group facilities rarely
have this as an option. But if you have control over the selection of your
meeting venue, it's worth the effort to see if you can find a suitable space,
which also has an opportunity for break time outside.

Take a look at the Energy Changing exercises in this chapter, find a few that
resonate with you. Try them out. Make them your own. Create new ones.
And, of course, have fun!

Ball Toss

I always include a NERF ball or something lightweight that I can toss around when I'm running a session for clients or consumers. It's the perfect little way to raise the energy of folks weary from sitting too long and it brings a smile to faces, too. Depending upon how you use it, you might also gather new ideas or insights, because the physical act of tossing the ball around tends to push the self-censor aside.

Energy Changer

5 minutes

Easy

Set Up Time:	15 seconds
Run Time:	3–5 minutes
Sharing:	spontaneous
Team Size:	groups of any size as long as you have the space
Materials Needed:	a colorful lightweight ball like a NERF ball

How to Do It

Let's get everybody standing up and come together in a fairly close circle so we're not too spread out. We'll just start tossing the ball back and forth to each other and as you toss the ball offer an _____ (*idea, an association to whatever you are working on, a feeling, or a belief, etc.*).

Call a stop when everyone has participated and you sense the group is more energized and relaxed.

Option

Write up the verbal contributions if you like.

Your Experiments and Notes

Mood Music

Don't be shy about incorporating your personal passions into the work
designs you create. You may have noticed that music is one of my passions,
so of course I weave music into qualitative research and client team ideation
whenever appropriate. Often I arrange for a CD/DVD player in my meeting
or session room so that I can use it whenever I feel the team needs a mood
change, or I want to get participants in the right mood for thinking about a
task, or I want to intentionally inspire imagination and ideas.

Energy Changer, Connection-Maker

5+ minutes

Prep Time (for pre-selecting appropriate music)

Easy

I'll cover all three approaches here.

Set Up Time:	1 minute; be sure to check in advance how to use the equipment and adjust the sound levels
Run Time:	as long as you wish
Sharing:	if appropriate to your intention
Team Size:	groups of any size
Materials Needed:	your selected music and a player/speakers, paper and pencil or pen for participants

How to Do It

For general background or mood setting

Pre-select music that relates to your task. For example, in a project on automotive cleaning products, I created a tape of travel and road music with
selections ranging from country to rock. For research on new pizza offer-
ings, we played a collection of old Italian Pop standards like "That's Amore."
And for a green marketing strategic session I found quirky tunes including
Sesame Street's "It's Not Easy Being Green." Putting this material together can
be a hoot in itself!

If you have the music playing softly in the background as participants
enter the meeting space, it immediately sets the right ambiance. When you
get down to work, turn the volume down, but turn it up again, not too loud,
if you run individual or small team exercises. Don't over-use your music or
it can become distracting.

Mood changers

I have created several CDs that contain a variety of mood specific music, including high octane African drumming, new age relaxation sounds, children's lullabies, sultry jazz and blues. Whenever I feel the team needs an energy change I cue up the right piece of music and let it play in the background for a few minutes.

Connection-makers

Music is a great creative lubricant, so it can be used very effectively to help individuals and teams relax, recall memories, conjure up images, and use their imaginations to think about ideas. When that is your intention you might want to play one or more snippets of music (perhaps themed to your task, as described earlier) and use a script such as the following:

> And now I'm going to play a little music for a few minutes. I'll invite you to close your eyes and listen and jot down some words of whatever images, memories or beginning ideas come to mind . . .

> *Then turn off the music.*

> And now I'd like you to look at your note pads and see if you can tease out some beginning ideas that relate to our task. Don't worry about them being perfect ideas, starting points are fine.

> *Have participants share whatever they wrote and invite everyone in the group to build on the starting points.*

Your Experiments and Notes

Lightning Round

When I studied acting in college we used to run a "lightning rehearsal" to quickly mark transitions from one actor to another and entrances and exits. It was a great way to run through a whole scene very quickly and memorize key elements. I've taken that concept and applied it to a variety of different facilitation modes. I use it most often with clients when debriefing a phase of research like a focus group. It's particularly helpful to use when people are tired and suffering fanny fatigue from sitting in the back room for hours. I'll describe that use and you can imagine how you might apply it in another setting, e.g., as a fast, stand up, mini-brainstorming session.

**Energy Changer,
Connection-
Maker**

10–15 minutes

Easy

Set Up Time:	30 seconds
Run Time:	10–15 minutes
Sharing:	fast, per person
Team Size:	groups of any size
Materials Needed:	flip chart and markers

How to Do It

Let's get everybody standing up and do a Lighting Debrief of what we just heard and observed. No censoring, I just want to quickly capture _____ (whatever you are going after, e.g., insights, key learnings, ahas!, surprises, implications).

Tip

Set up pair teams so that they can discuss ideas back and forth and feel less self-conscious about sharing what they have come up with.

Your Experiments and Notes

Quacks

Try this fast, competitive exercise with research participants or client teams as a quick mood changer and energy raiser. It will also give you insights about which members of your team are lateral thinkers.

Energy Changer

5 minutes

Easy

Set Up Time:	30 seconds
Run Time:	3+ minutes
Team Size:	groups of any size
Materials Needed:	paper and pen or pencil for each participant

How to Do It

How many "ducks" can you name in a minute? Get out a clean sheet of paper and quickly list as many as you can.

Give the group a minute, walk around, and scan their notes to make sure everyone has at least a few. If not, extend the time to 2 minutes, or, remind them that the word can be interpreted differently. (Don't write the word up on a board.)

Call a stop and ask people to tell you how many "ducks" they came up with. See who has the most "ducks" listed (and give praise) and then ask people to give you examples of what they had on their list. Of course you'll hear "mallards" and maybe "decoy ducks," but if you hear "conductor" or "duct tape," you know you've got some creative folks in your midst!

You can quickly debrief the exercise to make points about creative thinking, and that there isn't one "right answer" in this session.

Try this with other words that can lend themselves to creative misinterpretation.

Your Experiments and Notes

_____

_____

_____

_____

_____

_____

_____

Sentence Relay

This will bring a little lighthearted competition and humor to a meeting, whether with clients or research participants. It will get the blood moving, so it's most appropriate for participants who are comfortable with a little exercise.

Energy Changer

<5 minutes

Easy

Set Up Time:	1–2 minutes
Run Time:	under 3 minutes
Team Size:	4–10 people per team
Materials Needed:	2 (or more) standing easels with flip-chart paper and markers; stopwatch or clock; enough space for team members to "run" to the easels

How to Do It

Divide your group into two or more teams with no fewer than four on a team. Have the teams stand in lines some distance from the easels (10 feet or more if possible).

Write the same single word on each flip chart and cover it up so the word won't be seen until you are ready to do the exercise. It can be any word. I generally use a noun that has no apparent relationship to the task we are working on, for example, "salmon."

Now we're going to do a kids' game to get our energy up. I'm going to reveal a word on each flip chart and then each person will run up to the easels and add just one word. The only rule is that the word you add lead to the creation of a full sentence that's grammatically correct. We're going to do this for exactly _____ (*1 minute or longer, your choice and depending upon the size of the team and the size of the room*). Then I'm going to call a stop, and we'll see which team has created the best sentence.

Each participant runs up to the easel, writes a word and passes the marker on to the next person. Cheering and hollering is encouraged! At the end, the teams decide who has won.

Your Experiments and Notes

Baseball Stories (or other sports stories)

Baseball is deeply ingrained in the American culture. And even if you're not particularly a sports enthusiast, I find that everyone has at least a couple of fond memories or stories relating to the game.

I was kicking off a spring QRCA Chapter meeting recently which was going to feature two presentations; we had framed it as a "Doubleheader." In keeping with the motif, I asked meeting participants to go around the room introducing themselves and giving a short story about baseball in their lives. I said, "I grew up in Brooklyn, we were big fans of the underdogs, the Mets." (That got whoops and hollers from a couple of people in the group.) "Then I lived in Boston for many years and my loyalties switched to the Red Socks." (That got more whoops and hollers!) "And now I live in New Jersey and have divided loyalties." That got nods as others have moved around, too.

What was fascinating was that even though person after person said, "Oh, I'm not really a sports fan," each had a tasty, vivid tale to tell. Even the guest who grew up in Singapore could relate. Most important to me was how the energy in the room palpably changed. Everyone smiled, participated, was energized and enthused and ready to hear the presentations!

Energy Changer Connection-Maker

10+ minutes

Easy

Set Up Time:	30 seconds
Run Time:	under 1 minute per person
Team Size:	groups of 5–20 people
Materials Needed:	none

How to Do It

Let's go around the room and briefly share a little story about baseball. Even if you're not especially a sports fan, I bet you have a little nugget to share about the game.

Your Experiments and Notes

Tip

As moderator/ facilitator, briefly model the exercise. If people are stuck, you can broaden it to other sports stories. And don't let the women opt out of the exercise! You might also add in a cheer, encouraging word, or clap that signals that this is a lighthearted exchange, not serious business for the moment.

WordSalad

This exercise is essentially a word association game, but conducted with a bit of a meditative or dramatic flair depending upon how and when you want to use it. I've done this in a client team ideation session, sitting on the floor in the middle of a room. I've also done it standing up at a flip chart. Similar to Mind Mapping, it's great for having a team capture their connections, beginning ideas, threads, directions, or perceptions quickly, without censoring, and then you can go back to areas and probe or develop more fully.

Overall Tip: This exercise is all about getting into the rhythm of the words. You'll see what I mean in the directions below.

Energy Changer, Connection-Maker

10 minutes

Moderate

Set Up Time:	1–2 minutes
Run Time:	5 minutes or longer if you wish
Team Size:	any size group
Materials Needed:	flip-chart paper and a few different colored markers

How to Do It

I'm going to sketch out two different ways to set this up, both of which are Energy Changers. The first is a "meditative" exercise; the second is an energy raiser.

Meditative Set Up

We're going to do a little reflection and free associating next, and to get us in the right frame of mind, I'd like you to close your eyes for a minute, and take a few gentle, slow breaths. If you notice any tension anywhere in your body, breathe into that place and try to let it relax.

Energy Raiser Set Up

We're going to do a fast-free associating exercise next, so I'd like everyone to stand up for a couple of minutes.

Running the Exercise

Now I'm going to say a word (*start with a word that is clearly related to your task*) and I'm going to ask you to call out the first word that comes to your mind without censoring. We'll keep doing that for a few minutes and see what we come up with.

Tip

As facilitator, do the exercise along with the group. Close your eyes and perhaps make an audible sigh as you exhale. When you feel relaxed, hopefully after 3 or 4 breaths, it's time to run the exercise.

Write your first word in the center of the flip chart paper. As you hear someone offer the first associated word—whether or not you get the association doesn't matter—just write it down somewhere else on the paper. Then say that word out loud and wait for a response. Jot that word down somewhere on the paper and keep repeating the exercise. Hear a word from a member of the group, you repeat it and write it down, wait for another word, repeat it and write it down. If you've set this up as a meditative exercise, the words will come slowly, in a relaxed manner. You can control the rhythm with your breathing in the group. If you've set it up as a fast-paced word association, be ready to write the words quickly and dramatically. Use different colored markers for each word if you can. After the exercise has run for a few minutes you will feel that the connections are starting to run out. That's the time to call a stop. Invite the group to look at what has been created, a "WordSalad" because the words are scattered all over the flip chart. No doubt you will see themes or ideas that you want to explore further with a follow up activity.

Your Experiments and Notes

Build a Machine

This is an exercise that I learned in college days in a theater workshop and I've used it successfully in a number of client sessions devoted to idea generation and development. It raises the energy of a team, can often lead to fluency with ideas and it's a lot of fun. If the thought of doing something physical and improvisational makes you queasy you might skip this one; then again, I'll explain how easy it is and encourage you to experiment.

Energy Changer, Connection-Maker

12–15 minutes

Moderate

Set Up Time:	2 minutes
Run Time:	about 5+ minutes
Sharing:	5 minutes to debrief
Team Size:	groups of 5–12 people
Materials Needed:	a room with a large enough cleared space for your group to move around and participate and a space that is soundproof so that you don't have to be concerned about disturbing others

How to Do It

We have been working together in a conceptual way and now we're going to get out of our heads for a few minutes and try something fun and kinesthetic. We are going to build a machine together, one person at a time. I'm going to start and model; you'll see that I can make a fool of myself! In a moment I'm going to get in the center of the room and make a simple, repetitive movement and sound.

Now once I get started, don't leave me hanging there too long, I'd like you each to come on in and add to the machine with whatever movement, and sounds too, if you like. Let's try to get everyone involved and I'll call a stop when we are complete.

Tip

Do something easy that you can sustain for at least 3 minutes while everyone else on the team gets a chance to jump in and join the activity!

Now, in case you are having trouble visualizing this, I'll describe what happens. I'm likely to stand in the middle and move my arms in a wide arc from right to left and make a "swooshing" sound. Usually there is an awkward 60 seconds, then a brave soul gets into the action and connects with my swinging arms by going under and over mine, and then someone else gets in, and everyone follows suit pretty quickly. It can get loud and raucous.

Do encourage everyone to join, but don't force anyone. Let the exercise go as long as you like but certainly less than 5 minutes. Then be sure to discuss the exercise and quickly gather what people thought and experienced. You can embellish points about collaboration, listening, cooperation, creativity, etc. You might also find that people are naturally tying it back to something about the creative task you were working on.

Your Experiments and Notes

Move It!

The inspiration for this exercise came from two sources: a theater workshop, and a marvelous section from Jean Houston's *A Passion for the Possible*. She writes of African tribes who develop strategies for solving problems by dancing, singing, drawing in the sand, and imagining solutions. This exercise invites participants to use the whole body to express ideas and connections. Similar to the *Build a Machine* exercise (page 52), it's something that I've used with client teams, more so than consumer teams, especially when the energy has started to flag. It's great for positioning, or articulating benefits in new ways.

Energy Changer, Connection-Maker

10–15 minutes

Moderate

Set Up Time:	2 minutes
Run Time:	about 8+ minutes
Sharing:	5 minutes to debrief
Team Size:	groups of 5–12 people
Materials Needed:	a room with a large enough cleared space for your group to move around and participate and a space that is soundproof so that you don't have to be concerned about disturbing others

How to Do It

Let's get up and form a large circle and do a little movement exercise to help us think differently about this task. Here's the way this game works: Think about what this product (*or service*) offers to users and then we will go around the circle expressing that (*benefit*) with a physical movement, and a sound if you like. I'll model and then I'll ask you all to mimic what you see. Then I'll trade places with someone else in the group who will come up to the center of this circle and morph the earlier movement into his or her own expression, and so on. Don't explain what you are trying to convey, just let the movements of your body do it. And don't worry about how you look, it's just for fun and we'll see later if it triggers some ideas as well.

Tip

As moderator/facilitator, you have to be the first one to do the exercise and others will follow. Don't force someone to participate if they don't want to.

Here's an example from a session on food wraps. A person comes into the center and wraps her arms tightly around her shoulders, hugging herself. The rest of the group mimics the action. Then the person in the center nods that she is selecting a male participant in the group who has mimicked her movement well to trade places with her. The guy moves to the center of the circle and jumps up and down flaring hands wide open several times, accompanied by gleeful shouts. Everyone else in the circle follows suit. The center person selects someone else and nods for that person to trade places, and so on.

Now you might wonder about the meaning behind the movements. It's interesting but we usually communicate very well in an activity like this. The first woman conveyed the tightness of the wrap; the second guy, the freshness of the food, bursting with flavor because it's so well protected by the wrap.

After you run the exercise for a few minutes so that ideally everyone participates, it's a good idea to debrief and capture the thinking behind the movements (if it's not obvious) and the connections to the task at hand.

Your Experiments and Notes

Additional Energy Changers Experiments and Observations

Connection-Makers

The heart
of idea
generation

The Truthsayers section is primarily about getting insights from the minds, hearts, and behaviors of research subjects, whether they are consumers, customers, shoppers, or business professionals. This Connection-Makers section is primarily about getting new ideas. It's a deliberately broad term. "Connections" reflect the way the brain operates, growing new nerve cells or neurons, which are connections that resemble branches on a tree. The branches send and receive signals. The more branches there are, the more paths by which a neuron can send and receive information. The good news is that your brain doesn't stop growing and making new connections as an adult. When you learn new things, you make new connections. This is one of the reasons I love the work that I do. I am constantly immersed in new areas and learning new things.

Connection-making is about weaving imagination, insight, and experiences together. In the exercises in this chapter we'll "borrow powers" from animals, use collages: (pictures, words, videos or 3-dimensional toys), and look for nuggets of ideas, create stories, and venture into "other worlds" to find parallels.

At the heart of many of these activities is a simple, three-step process. We select an object/word/example (which may or may not have any direct relation to the task), we explore and generate raw material, and then we make a connection between that raw material and the problem we are looking to solve. It's not all that mysterious. It's kind of the way our brains work naturally. You probably have noticed that when you are wrestling with a problem that you are just as likely to come up with possibilities or "ahas!" in the shower, in the gym, at the breakfast table, in the car, on a walk, or wherever. The ideas can surface when you least expect them, when you are not "working" on the problem. That in a nutshell is what we are doing here with connection-making exercises, just making the process visible and speedy.

While the tools are easy to use, there is an art to using them. There are a host of "soft" skills and attitudes that are also the skills necessary to be a great convener, moderator, or facilitator of any kind. Exuding personal warmth and demonstrating great listening skills are essential. Also to be good at facilitating connection-making exercises requires a spirit of experimentation, willingness to take risks, being flexible and able to think fast on your feet, changing direction if an exercise isn't working the way you imagined it would. Confidence in your ability to carry off an exercise and faith in your participants is essential.

I have learned to trust the process, even if I can't anticipate what ideas may come from an activity. I have many years' experience that has proven to me that I will get results. It just comes from doing the work, there's no shortcut here. In *Outliers*, Malcolm Gladwell writes of mastery as requiring 10,000 hours of practice. I'm sure I've put in that much time in this craft.

Lastly and very important to the creative process is curiosity and well-rounded experiences. I read voraciously—not just materials that are germane to the categories or industries in which I work—but I keep up on a wide range of matters from culture and the arts to science, technology, and finance. I make it a point to take "creative inspiration days" to wander museums, learn news things, chat with people in other fields. I have to do this because that's where the creativity and innovation happen. It's the cross connections and the synergy that are exciting and lead to breakthroughs.

The literature of invention is filled with stories of these cross connections. Wilson Greatbatch, an electrical engineer, invented the medical cardiac pacemaker and a corrosion-free lithium battery to power it. He noticed that the problem with failing hearts was both a biological problem and an electrical one.

Swiss amateur mountaineer George de Mestral liked to take his faithful companion on a walk in the woods and noticed how annoying it was to get the burrs off his dog's fur and his own pants. Curiosity made him take a look at these prickly burrs under the microscope, and he got the inspiration for a new type of fastener to replace the zipper. He invented a unique two-sided fastener—one with stiff hooks like burrs and the other with soft loops like the fabric of his pants. Velcro was born years later through George's persistence and hard work.

I'm also struck by a fascinating story of invention in the world of gastronomy. Award-winning, avant-garde chef and restaurateur, Grant Achatz, looks to other disciplines and technologies normally not part of the chef's repertoire in order to cook, shape and manipulate ingredients to create unique and provocative tastes and effects. This led him to partner with a company in the medical industry that makes temperature control devices to create the inverse of a pancake griddle: a device that freezes foods that normally don't freeze, instead of heating them. One of the dishes from Grant's "anti-griddle" is an herb-infused frozen olive oil lollipop.

Wild stuff, to be sure! And as these examples show, it's useful and profitable to explore. I encourage you to explore the activities in this chapter and have productive fun creating new connections and ideas.

Analogy Safari

This is a good exercise for combating mid-afternoon fatigue and it will help inspire new connections too. I've used this with client teams for a variety of meeting agendas—strategic, new products, or positioning. It's very easy to set up. It works best in a venue like a hotel meeting room or conference room where you can send your team out to "hunt" for items.

Connection-Maker, Energy Raiser

15 minutes

Easy

Set Up Time:	1 minute
Run Time:	10 minutes
Sharing:	30 seconds per person
Team Size:	groups of any size as long as you have the time
Materials Needed:	flip-chart paper and a colored marker

How to Do It

You probably won't pre-plan this exercise but will notice a time when it would be good to get your team up and moving. You will have to think on your feet and come up with one or more "themes" or areas for participants to gather "analogical" materials.

Place a sheet of flip-chart paper on the floor or on a large tabletop.

For the next _____ (5 or 10 minutes, don't give them more time!) I want you to get out of this room and hunt for items that in some way represent _____ (pick a theme from whatever your task is).

For example, for a client working on premium beverages we asked participants to find examples of "quality" or "premium" from worlds unrelated to foods and beverages. They collected items including an American Express Gold Card, a luxurious bath towel, and a glossy vacation destination magazine.

Bring your items back with you. If you can't physically bring them back to the workspace, make a sketch, or write the words on sticky notes and place them on this flip chart canvas.

When all participants have returned, keep the energy up by having them stand up as you field the exercise. As facilitator, point to an item and ask whoever brought it to the room to briefly tell you about it. When you have heard about all the items, let participants sit down and give them a few minutes to see what ideas the exercise sparks. Write these on flip-chart paper. At the end of session be sure to return the items that were collected to their rightful owners!

Your Experiments and Notes

Doodling

My guess is that just about everyone doodles at times, so here is an easy way to make doodling pave the way for idea generation. You can do this spontaneously with just about any group of research participants or client team.

Set Up Time:	1 minute
Run Time:	5+ minutes
Sharing:	30 seconds per person
Team Size:	groups of any size
Materials Needed:	paper and pen or colored markers or crayons for each participant

How to Do It

Let's turn our attention away from _____ (*whatever your topic of discussion was*) and play for a few minutes, doing something that you probably like to do any way. I'm going to ask you to just doodle. Literally, fill up a page with lines, colors at random. Now if your doodling starts to look like something in particular, make it more abstract. I'm going to give you about a minute to doodle.

After a minute call a stop and ask participants to pass their doodles to the person on the left.

Now I'd like you to pick up on the doodle you have just received and add to it, embellish it.

Give participants a minute to do this and then call another stop.

One more time. Pass the doodle to the person on your left to continue adding to the doodle.

Call a stop, and then . . .

Now instead of passing the doodle further, I'd like you to look closely at what you have. Turn it sideways or upside down. Contained in this doodle is a thread, a beginning idea for _____ (*our challenge*). The great Michelangelo believed that the sculpture was already inside the marble; his carving helped release it. In similar fashion, your job is to find the ideas that reside inside the doodle—make a connection between something you see in this doodle and the task. I'll start collecting your ideas in a minute.

Tip

If your participants are reluctant to get started, you can model this on a flip chart, making big bold lines and strokes of color.

Give participants a minute and start fielding the ideas. If someone is "uninspired" they can look at your doodle (if you modeled the exercise), or look over at someone else's doodle. The ideas that emerge may be tenuous. Through probing and encouragement, try to get people to build on them and tease out as many ideas as you can. Even if you don't get a lot of clearly usable ideas, the exercise will serve as a good mental refresher before other activities and aspects of your discussion.

Your Experiments and Notes

Short Stories

This exercise brings out the inner Steven King or Danielle Steele. It's easy to do; I've used it with consumer and client teams at various stages in a session. It's great for providing some seemingly random raw material as a springboard for ideation. This exercise often triggers a healthy dose of laughter, and sometimes can help participants articulate an inner truth. Many years after I had first started using this exercise I took a weekend writers' workshop with the poet and NPR commentator Andrei Codrescu, known for *The Exquisite Corpse: a Journal of Books and Ideas*. One of the fascinating activities he had us do was a collaborative poem-building exercise such as this one. The eerily wonderful result was published in a journal for participants.

Connection-Maker, Truthsayer

10-12 minutes

Easy

Set Up Time:	1 minute
Run Time:	5 minutes
Sharing:	1 minute per person
Team Size:	small to medium-size groups
Materials Needed:	paper and pen for each participant

How to Do It

Here's your turn to be _____ *(fill in your favorite author)*. I'm going to give you a first line of a short story.

You make up the line. I use words like:
"She opened the door . . . ," or
"There was a dark night . . . ," (which can be interpreted as "knight,")
or the old standby, "Once upon a time. . . . "

Write this first line on the top of a sheet of paper. It helps if you can write fairly legibly. Now you add a line or two to begin a good story.

After a minute, call a stop and have people pass their sheets to the person on their right.

Now, you have the job of building upon this story. I'm going to give you a minute to do that.

At the end of a minute call a stop, and again, have people pass their sheets to the person on the right. You can have them do this as many times as you like but usually three passes is sufficient. You just want to see that there are at least three to four sentences on a sheet so there is enough material to work with.

For the last pass:

> I'd like you to wrap up the story. And then pass it to the person on your right. Now you have each received a tasty short story. Take a minute to read through it, and if you can't read a word don't worry, just guess. And if you like, you can imagine writing a final line to the story. Then I'd like you to see what your story might suggest in terms of an idea for our topic.

Give participants a minute to collect their thoughts and then capture their ideas on flip charts. Encourage them to just give you the ideas and not read through the whole story. However, if you have time, or if you have a team that seems stymied about how to begin, you can ask a volunteer to read one of the stories aloud and then have the whole group use that story as a springboard for an idea. It's always helpful if you, as facilitator, can come up with a quick example on your own to model the type of connection-making you are looking for.

Your Experiments and Notes

Trees
(aka Mind Maps)

Many researchers and facilitators use Mind Maps as a way to capture ideas, perceptions, associations, attitudes, and more in free flowing diagrams. By capturing ideas quickly on a large easel sheet or white board, we give participants permission to be expressive and creative, and to keep the self-censor at bay. You can use this approach for connection-making and brainstorming in many situations, whether your objectives are strategic or tactical. There are even software platforms available for those who want to do this activity online. After a Mind Map is generated, you can go back and look more closely to delve into potential inter-relationships or find ways to organize the output.

Another way that I like to frame this exercise is by conceptualizing it as creating "trees." I start by drawing the outline of a large tree and roots, and add branches and leaves containing the participant's comments (ideas, perceptions, associations, etc.). Trees promote lateral thinking and also some degree of focus. You can quickly create several trees, each one on a different aspect of your project task.

**Connection-Maker,
Idea Developer**

5-10+ minutes

Easy

Set Up Time:	1 minute
Run Time:	5–10 minutes or more
Sharing:	everyone participates in rapid fire
Team Size:	groups of any size
Materials Needed:	large flip-chart paper and colored marker

How to Do It

As moderator/facilitator, start by drawing a large, simple sketch of the trunk of a tree, roots, and a ground line. You label the trunk to indicate the area of focus. For example, on a project related to shoppers' retail experiences, we labeled a tree trunk "In-Store Promotions," and participants' associations, connections, ideas, etc. each became a branch of the tree. Builds on a particular aspect became buds or leaves of the tree. We labeled another tree trunk "Customer Service" and captured on its branches, buds, and leaves our shoppers' attitudes and perceptions of their delights and disappointments at the retail venues under discussion.

After you have collected this material you can direct your participants to take a closer look and see what new ideas, themes, or directions have been suggested and capture these "next generation" comments in a more traditional listing.

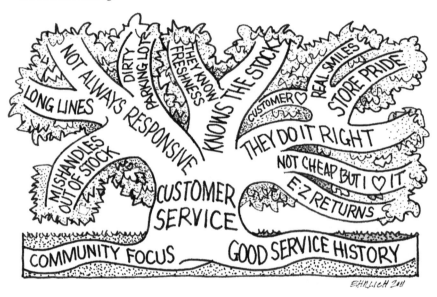

Your Experiments and Notes

SCAMPERing

Connection-
Maker

10–30 minutes

Easy

I learned the SCAMPER technique in my early days as an innovation consultant while attending a Creative Problem Solving Institute (CPSI) conference and it's long been a staple exercise. The technique of using idea-sparking questions was attributed to Alex Osborne, but the specific acronym of SCAMPER has been attributed to others—Bob Eberle or Bob Earle; the literature is murky. Thank you to whoever's "baby" this is. I've adapted it in my own fashion.

This is fun and easy to use with clients or consumers. It can inspire a long list of ideas in a brief period of time. I find it's good at the early stages of an innovation process with a broadly defined task or problem to solve, e.g., generate new ideas for floor cleaning products. At home, I keep SCAMPER in mind when creating new recipes.

There are many ways you can use SCAMPER. The simplest is to write the word SCAMPER with a description of the questions or prompts on a large flip chart and let participants refer to the chart whenever they are stuck.

Another approach is to assign your team members one of the SCAMPER elements and have them focus on coming up with ideas based on that specific question.

I'm going to illustrate a third way to use this which gets a bit of physical movement into the mix, so that participants are literally *scampering* from place to place as they are brainstorming.

Set Up Time:	3 minutes
Run Time:	7–30 minutes (one minute per SCAMPER element or letter)
Team Size:	groups of any size
Materials Needed:	7 flip-chart sheets and markers or white boards spread around the room

How to Do It

Ahead of time, post SCAMPER on a flip chart or white board. When you are ready to run the exercise, reveal the acronym and describe the questions you'll use to spark, stimulate, and trigger ideas. These are the types of questions that I use to describe SCAMPER; I tend to vary them a bit based on the nature of the challenge we are working on.

Substitute

Which ingredients, components, parts of a product or process can be substituted or changed?

Combine

Which ingredients, components, parts of a product or process can be combined to make something unique?

Adapt

Which ingredients, components, parts of a product or process could be adapted or changed to solve part of the problem or change the nature of the task?

Tip

Keep the energy moving briskly.

Modify, Magnify or Miniaturize

Which part of the situation could be enlarged or diminished, or what happens if the product or process is enlarged or diminished?

Put to Other Purposes

How can we take this product/process and use it differently or put it in a different context?

Eliminate

What if we removed an ingredient, a component of the product or process?

Reverse or Rearrange

What can we reverse or rearrange? (This is a great prompt for a packaging assignment: Can the "top" of the product become the "bottom" for example?)

Put one word from the acronym at the top of seven flip-chart pages spread out around your workspace. Ask each participant to start at a different flip chart and begin quickly writing up whatever ideas come to mind without censoring their thoughts. After a few minutes call a stop and have participants rotate to the next flip chart. They should look over the ideas before them, then build or add new ideas to the sheet. Continue doing this for as long as you like and as long as the ideas are flowing. If someone gets stuck at a sheet, that's okay, just have them rotate to the next one. About five minutes before you want to end the exercise, ask the person situated at each flip chart to review the entire list of ideas before them and check the ones that they think are most "intriguing" or "unique" (or whatever criteria you want to use). Go around the room reading those selected ideas aloud.

Variation

If your meeting space doesn't allow you to move about easily, assign each person a starting point and note that word on the top of his or her own note pads. Brainstorm as individuals or pairs for a few minutes, and then ask them to pass their work sheets on to the person(s) on the right. You get the same kind of output without the physical movement.

Your Experiments and Notes

Google Grazing & Blog Browsing

When I first started running innovation sessions for client teams I would often go through my library of articles and pull out a dozen that I thought would provide relevant information or interesting stretch to the thought process. I'd copy the articles, mail them to the team leader and ask her to distribute amongst session members prior to the engagement. Participants liked this and commented that it was a good springboard for ideas. These days that process is so much easier!

Now as prelude to an innovation session I create a meeting invitation that includes a menu of pre-session activities. I generally put this exercise on the list. It helps to give direction by providing a few sample websites or blogs for people to start with. My aim is often to identify topic areas or sites that I think my client teams may not have on their typical radar screen. For example, when working on a repositioning project related to food freshness, I asked my clients to explore parallels of "freshness" in non-food areas and I included some listings about personal care products like shampoos.

Connection-Maker

~30 minutes as homework assignment

~20+ minutes discussion in session

Easy

Set Up Time:	pre-session, to craft a homework invitation
Run Time:	2+ minutes per person
Team Size:	groups of any size
Materials Needed:	flip chart & marker or whiteboard to capture ideas

How to Do It

To get people oriented, it helps if you as facilitator pre-select sites for participants to peruse, particularly areas that you believe will provide useful information, novelty, voice of the customer, or analogous situations to the client's task.

Instruct participants to go beyond your suggested list and peruse a variety of websites and blogs. Take notes of what they find intriguing and be prepared to talk about at least one or two nuggets or ideas that have been inspired by the exercise.

Your Experiments and Notes

Option

Since most professionals travel with laptops or other mobile devices with access to the web you can do this activity live, in session, if you are willing to allocate that additional time.

Tip

To shortcut your preparation time, it helps if you have bookmarked a number of places that you have found to provide rich content and that will help inspire the client team.

Linguistics Wordplay
(five cool things to do for name generation)

Naming things—products, services, brands, (or babies!)—can be one of the most challenging tasks. When I've been called upon to help a client come up with a new name, it's not unusual for us to generate hundreds of name candidates, which the client will then pare down to a short list of candidates that they favor and that fit their business criteria. Even though we will integrate preliminary trademark searches periodically throughout the generative phase, the biggest challenge is often getting legal clearance in all the business or trade categories and countries that the client is interested in.

Connection-Maker

30 minutes

Moderate

While I'm not going to do justice in this brief description to the whole complex process of naming, there are five linguistic approaches that should be part of a creative facilitator's toolbox: **Alliteration, Assonance, Consonance, Onomatopoeia,** and **Portmanteau**. I typically use all of these exercises and several others (including *Everything Sounds Better in Italian*) within a name-generation session of one or two days. I can count on each technique yielding 10 to 50 or more name candidates, depending upon how long I want to play out the exercise. I usually get best results by running lots of naming exercises of 30 minutes or less throughout a day.

The basic approach is to illustrate the linguistic concept with examples in the marketplace, and a thought-sparker of your own that relates to your specific project. Don't get nervous if it takes a minute or two for the ideas to start to flow. You might suggest that participants take a quiet moment using their own note pads to come up with some possibilities before opening up the floor to the whole team. You can also set up pair teams or triads to come up with ideas first and then share with the whole group.

Once you start capturing name candidates on flip charts, or white boards, invite participants to build on each other's ideas.

Here's a description of each linguistic approach:

Alliteration refers to repetition of a particular sound, usually in the first letter. Alliterative names are usually fun to say. Examples are Dunkin' Donuts and Best Buy.

Assonance is repetition of vowel sounds, but the surrounding consonants are different. YouTube, Reese's Pieces and FedEx are good examples.

Consonance is repetition of final consonants of important words or accented syllables. The clothing brand OshKosh B'gosh can be considered an example, although other linguistic elements are in play as well.

Onomatopoeia refers to a word whose sound suggests the meaning. An example from the world of animals is "meow," from brands: Whirlpool.

Portmanteau is a blend of two or more words that combines their meanings. *Verizon* seems to be a portmanteau of *veritas* (Latin for "truth") and *zon* (from "horizon" in English).

Your Experiments and Notes

Everything Sounds Better in Italian

I love to travel, which is a good thing, since much of my work is "on the road." My most delightful travel experiences are abroad. I relish the opportunity to immerse myself in different cultures, food, and language. I find that I can often mimic the flavor and intonation of another language even if I can hardly speak a word. Italian is one of those languages that I find so musically pleasing. Doesn't everything sound better with an Italian accent? It's in a spirit of playfulness that I created this exercise many years ago when I was working with a client to help them name a new line of confectionery products. Using this approach, we came up with a long list of mouth-pleasing name candidates.

Connection-Maker

under 30 minutes

Moderate

Set Up Time:	1 minute
Run Time:	10 minutes
Sharing:	20+ minutes
Team Size:	groups of any size
Materials Needed:	a variety of dictionaries — Italian, Spanish, French, Latin, German, Dutch

How to Do It

Put a variety of foreign language dictionaries out on a table for participants to browse.

Ask participants to start with one dictionary and first "thumb through" at random.

Then ask them to check translations for some of the names, themes, positioning ideas they have already generated in English, and make notes on their own pads of whatever sparks their interest.

Then suggest that they combine elements of words, resulting in name candidates that sound appealing and seem appropriate to the product/category, although they may be "nonsensical" combinations, invented words or portmanteaus (which are based on blending two or more distinct words and combining their meanings).

Note

I've only done this exercise in languages that are more recognizable and familiar to English speaking teams. I think it would be too difficult to attempt this with Chinese, Arabic, and Russian dictionaries.

After you have given individuals or small teams some time to do this activity (about 10 minutes) have them report their ideas and name candidates to the full group, using their interpretation of the accent appropriate to that language. Then ask others to "build" or enhance the name possibilities. You can continue with several rounds of this game, each time having participants delve into a different dictionary.

In addition to the fun value of this game, it is effective because you might end up with names that can be more easily trademarked than English words would be.

Your Experiments and Notes

Playing with Paradox

I love working with "paradoxes" in research settings and client team ideation sessions. Paradoxes are apparent contradictions, where both "A" and "B" are true. They are intense, fighting truths, that when articulated, can help break through boundaries of thinking about a product, a brand, or a situation. This is the type of exercise that you can effectively use once the team is rolling a bit; it's not the first activity to try in a session.

For example, in an assignment to stimulate new language for advertising, I asked consumer teams to identify paradoxes about using their contact lens cleaning solutions and someone described her lens cleaners as "gentle toxicity." (Why? Because chemicals are necessary to sterilize lenses and get rid of protein build up, and yet the cleaners are not so strong as to damage the very thin, flexible plastic contact lens.)

In a brand revitalization assignment for a bioenergy company, our clients came up with "living decomposition" and "renewable disposables." And in a new messaging assignment for a premium coffee brand the team suggested "affordable luxury" and "complex simplicity" as hallmarks of their products and business.

Set Up Time:	1 minute
Run Time:	10+ minutes
Team Size:	individuals, or groups of any size
Materials Needed:	flip chart and markers

How to Do It

Be ready to give an example or two of your own to get the group started.

There are some interesting, contradictory elements inherent in our discussion about this _____ (brand, etc.). Let's capture them in succinct, two or three word phrases, like a book title. A good example is the book, *The Lonely Crowd*. As we go around the room, let's collect these paradoxes, and tell us a little about what you are thinking. You can take some liberties with language here. It's great when the paradoxes are not entirely apparent, but make us think more deeply about our _____ (brand, etc.).

Tips

Try to avoid "this vs. that" phrases, and encourage people to condense their paradox into a book title or short phrase. If they are stuck, you can have them work in pairs, since it's likely that one member will be more fluent at coming up with an example.

Collect the paradoxes on a flip chart and then ask participants to select one or two that intrigue them. Play out the exercise further by asking individuals or pair teams to work with the paradoxes to see where they might lead in terms of ideas or connections back to your task at hand.

Your Experiments and Notes

_____

_____

_____

_____

_____

_____

_____

_____

_____

_____

Percussive Jam

If you're comfortable with making music, this is not a difficult exercise, but if rhythm and music are not your thing, the exercise will require a little bravery to pull it off.

I remember clearly the first time I tried this. We were working with a client team (primarily marketers, product development and advertising people) in a B&B a few hours' drive from my home.

Our percussive jam turned out to be outstanding fun and very productive!

Our task was to come up with a portfolio of new ideas for ready-to-eat breakfasts. This session was the first in a series of efforts including follow-up consumer research, so in addition to achieving specific content results, it was critical to establish a strong foundation of trust, productivity, and fun.

I have a large collection of percussion instruments—drums of all sizes and types, rattles, cowbells, tambourines, and shakers, so I filled up my car with a dozen of these items thinking I might want to use them in some way, although I hadn't formulated a specific exercise. Our percussive jam was outstanding fun and very productive.

If you don't have a cache of instruments, you can pick up a number of inexpensive items at toy and novelty stores, or you can see if there are suitable items in your work room that can be called into play. Of course you want to make sure you are in a place where you can be noisy for a little while without disturbing others!

Connection-Maker, Team Builder, Energy Raiser

10+ minutes

Moderate

Set Up Time:	1 minute
Run Time:	10 minutes or more
Team Size:	groups of any size as long as you have the time, space and equipment
Materials Needed:	a variety of percussive instruments or "sticks," and hard surfaces that can be used as substitutes for drums and other similar instruments

How to Do It

Put a variety of instruments in the center of the room. If appropriate you might even want to sit on the floor and invite everyone to join you on the floor while you do this exercise.

We're not calling upon accomplished musicians here, but rather asking you to get into your natural kid's rhythm and play space. I'm going to start by picking up one of these instruments at random. I'll check it out, feel it in my hand, and see how it works, and I'm going to invite you all to do the same. Pick up an instrument that intrigues you, whether or not you've ever seen it before doesn't matter. Now in a minute I'm going to start beating out a little rhythm and as you feel moved, come join in. The rhythm will expand and change with each addition. It's what jazz musicians call jamming. We'll do this for a little bit and then see what we might take from this experience and weave into our work at hand.

Give participants a good 5 to 10 minutes to explore and create rhythm. You, as leader, can call a stop at any time or change the rhythm if you like. Otherwise you will likely have some moments when it sounds lovely, very musical, with people in synch, and at other times it may sound a bit *cacophonous*. (Now isn't that a cool onomatopoetic word? And also a great metaphor for what happens in the creative process!) Go with the flow. When you feel you have come to a good place to stop, call a stop. Let the group be silent for a moment to take in what transpired and then either invite them to see if they can build some ideas from the experience or just move onto your next area of focus. At some point during the session it would be good to debrief the experience and see what people thought of it.

Your Experiments and Notes

Get Fired!

Sometimes it's really hard to get a team to be speculative and creative. Perhaps this kind of thinking process is very different from the way they typically work, or their industry is extremely conservative, so that lateral thinking exercises are not encouraged. Here's an exercise that always seems to break through the resistance. It requires a little drama to pull off, and you, the facilitator, have to believe in your heart that you will get good results. You can use this with client or consumer teams on any task for which you are seeking ideas.

Connection-Maker

10+ minutes

Moderate

Set Up Time:	1 minute
Run Time:	10 minutes or more
Team Size:	small to medium-size groups
Materials Needed:	flip-chart paper and marker; pen and paper for participants

How to Do It

Now I want to give you permission to come up with some really novel _____ (*solutions, or whatever you are working toward*). For the next few minutes I'd like you to give me all those wild and crazy ideas that you never thought you could say out loud. They are the "get fired" ideas or the notions that are "illegal, immoral, or fattening" (*that usually gets a laugh*). The only caveat is that there has to be something in the idea that if it could be implemented, really would help _____ (*solve the problem, etc.*).

Let's get these ideas up quickly, without censoring. No one outside this room ever has to know about these ideas.

Keep the pace up with your energy and movement. Try to get at least one "Get Fired" idea from each person. If the team is reticent, model an idea just to get them started. After a few minutes, call a stop and go to the next phase.

Great, and now let's take these ideas and see where they might lead. I'd like each of you to select any one idea that you like and write it on your own pads, even if you can't imagine how you might implement it. Then huddle with a partner and talk through what you have, tossing ideas back and forth like ping-pong. See if you can come up with at least one idea that came from the "Get Fired" that is more feasible.

Tip

Before you leave this activity, you just might want to tear up the 'Get Fired' list and not put them in the final meeting notes. I've worked with some pharmaceutical and financial services clients who were uncomfortable if these raw notes were ever disseminated outside the room.

Listen in as people are talking and give them a couple of minutes to start making connections, then capture those "next generation" ideas on flip charts.

Your Experiments and Notes

Visit other Worlds (or Realms or Contexts)

I learned this analogical exercise when I worked at Synectics and I look at it as a faithful old friend. It works remarkably well with all types of participants—research subjects and client teams in just about any project in which we are seeking ideas. You can run the exercise fairly quickly by just pulling analogies from one realm or "world," but I often like to mix it up and ask participants to come up with multiple examples in different realms.

Connection-Maker

15–20 minutes or more

Moderate

There are five steps to the exercise:

You, as moderator/facilitator, will select a word, phrase, or idea that is germane to your task.

Then you select a "world" that seems to have no particular relationship to what you are working on.

Ask participants to give examples of that word or phrase or idea in the context of that unrelated world.

Ask participants to select one or more of the examples and think about what they might extract or connect back to the task at hand.

Capture participants' ideas, taking them as far as they will go.

Here are some examples of how I've put this exercise into play:

In a project with a food manufacturer looking for ways to have better impact at retail, one focal area for our thinking was to identify ideal shelf adjacencies or product partners. I wrote the words: "Perfect Partners" and asked participants to give examples from any worlds other than food. Their examples included Laurel and Hardy, shoes and socks, tennis racket and ball. These far afield examples helped the team make fresh connections and generate new ideas. It got the team thinking about how their foods fit into a healthy, active lifestyle and ways to promote this.

In a project with consumers on automotive cleaning products, we asked our research participants to come up with "examples of cleaning from the world of nature" (and heard things like rain), "examples of cleaning from the world of history" (and got examples like sandblasting old buildings), and "examples of cleaning from the world of foods" (and an example was fiber for internal cleaning). As you might imagine, this exercise really opens the mind to greater possibilities than if we just think about cleaning products in a traditional way.

Set Up Time:	1 minute
Run Time:	5–10+ minutes, depending upon how many examples and worlds you use
Sharing:	5–20+ minutes, depending on how many connections and ideas are generated
Team Size:	groups of any size
Materials Needed:	flip chart and markers; pen and paper for each participant

How to Do It

We are going to take a few minutes to step away from our task and get lost in other worlds. I'll bring you back later, and you will see how valuable this mind stretching exercise is! But first, I've written up this _____ (*word or phrase*) and I just want you to quickly give me examples of this _____ (*word or phrase*) in a different world (*write the world at top of a flip chart*).

Now I want you to select one or more of these examples and write them on your own note pads. Think about the example. What is the operating principle behind it? How does it "work"? Then take a minute to connect it back to our task and I'll collect your ideas.

Give participants time to make the leap from example to connection and then chart up their ideas. If they have trouble with this, provide an example of your own.

Your Experiments and Notes

_____

_____

_____

_____

_____

_____

_____

_____

_____

_____

_____

Tip

Try to fill up a page with examples. Have an example ready in your mind if you need to model. The examples don't have to be precise or correct; it's the connection that your participants make that counts.

If the team is having trouble coming up with examples in a world, switch to another. And yes, you have to be able to think on your feet in order to be successful.

Deconstruction

"Every act of creation is first an act of destruction." This striking quote is attributed to the artist Pablo Picasso, and is the inspiration for this next exercise,
which I first experienced many years ago from a Creative Problem Solving
Institute (CPSI) colleague, William Sturner. I don't remember exactly how
he did the exercise, but I've used my variation of it in numerous situations.
It's more appropriate for client teams than research participants, because a
fair amount of time is needed in order to get the full value of the exercise.
It's best suited for a task related to product improvements or line extension
ideas, and for re-positioning existing products.

   I used this recently with a storage products client who was looking to
bring "new news" to its existing product lines in two ways: by communicating its existing products' benefits in fresh ways, and by designing product
improvements.

**Connection-
Maker,
Idea Developer**

**15+ minutes
or more**

Moderate

Set Up Time:	3 minutes
Run Time:	10 minutes or more
Sharing:	1–2 minutes per team
Team Size:	this works well with groups of 6–12 persons
Materials Needed:	imagination only, or some sample products that are the focus of your task

How to Do It

Set up your group in pair teams or triads. It's particularly exciting if you can
combine different types of expertise within each team, such as a marketing
professional with an engineer.

   Here's the way I directed my clients:

   Select one of the items in your current line-up. Mentally take the item apart into its
   many different facets or elements (*for this project the items might have been locks,
   seams, glue, tabs, plastic strips, colors, etc.*). Examine the elements closely, as if you
   have never seen them before. Now mentally put the product back, and you can add or
   change just one element. Reconstruct the product with this new element and consider
   how it might change in function. Now you have a last opportunity to change it via the
   "magic wand." What have you ended up creating? Present your new product to the
   team, telling us what it is, and what the key benefit is.

In case you missed the elements in the script, the steps of this exercise are:

1. A product
2. Deconstruct it into its various components or elements
3. Examine thoroughly
4. Reconstruct it adding or changing only one element
5. Use a final pass of the magic wand for a further improvement
6. Re-present the new object and its benefit

Your Experiments and Notes

Creating ("Preferred") Futures

This is a powerful exercise that I've used hundreds of times with clients in a wide range of industries. Its best application is for strategic assignments where we want to uncover big themes, directions, and business platforms. I could certainly spend a half-day or more just on this exercise, but the practicalities of session time usually mean that we have to do the whole exercise in 60 to 90 minutes.

Connection-Maker

60–90+ minutes

Moderate

This is a small team exercise (preferably of mixed disciplines) where the teams imagine their company/division/brand etc., and the environment surrounding it at some point in the future. You as facilitator assign each team a different time frame, depending upon the appropriateness for your client and the project. For a pharmaceutical project, where it takes many years from concept to marketplace, I might assign one team a 5-year horizon, another 10 years, and ask the third to imagine the future 15 years hence. For a food company, which generally works much faster, the time frames for the exercise would more likely be 1 year, 3 years, and 5 years into the future.

Set Up Time:	3 minutes
Run Time:	at least 25 minutes for teams to work through their thinking
Sharing:	give teams 3 to 5 minutes each to present their thinking, and take as much time as you can to debrief and capture connections and ideas, ideally at least 30 minutes
Team Size:	groups of 8 or more, set up in smaller work teams of 3 to 5 participants
Materials Needed:	flip-chart paper, colored markers, any other stimuli you like

How to Do It

I tend not to give a lot of direction, but rather let the teams wrestle with the assignment and interpret it as they will; this brings more creativity to the process.

Here are two ways I tend to set it up. The first is a more literal approach using a "media front page." The second uses a metaphorical framework to imagine the future.

> In your small teams, create a "media front page" for your given time frame. You can envision that as *USA Today*, or the *New York Times*, or an online publication; you make that decision in your team. Then your job is to create the lead stories that you want to see that convey the big news of your _____ (*company, brand, division, etc.*), and what's going on in the "environment." The environment might include anything in

the world—politics, education, transportation, weather, technology, etc.—that might have some impact on your business. Include headlines, pictures, graphs, or whatever you deem necessary.

Or . . .

In your small teams, please draw a _____ (*building or vehicle, etc.*) in an environment _____ (*road, city, landscape, seascape, etc.*). The time frame is _____ (*1 year from now, 3 years, etc.*). Your _____ (*company, brand, division*) is represented by that _____ (*building, vehicle, etc.*).

Label all the key parts of your drawing: the components of the environment and the forces, positive or negative, that are impacting your _____ (*company, brand, division*).

Sharing

After teams have completed their work, let them present their thinking to the full group and give them a time limit, e.g., three minutes, to do so. Remind everyone to actively listen and tell them you will be capturing ideas afterward.

Making connections from the news stories, metaphors or analogies

First begin by asking team members what they notice in terms of overlapping themes, points of agreement, or disagreement. Then you can likely use the news stories, metaphors, or analogies to cull out corporate or brand strengths, weakness, competitive threats, opportunities, and ideas.

Sometimes what is most fascinating is what is *missing* from the drawings. I recall a project 20 years ago with a biotech company in which we used vehicles in an environment as the overarching framework. None of the teams' drawings included people! That missing element became the springboard for a rich discussion about how the company had to be more customer and consumer centric. The ultimate end users' lives could be dramatically improved by the research and projects that the firm was engaged in.

Your Experiments and Notes

Tip

Keep the teams' worksheets hanging up in the room as long as your meeting lasts because participants are likely to keep coming back and finding more insights and ideas that will inform later activities.

Competitive Products Olympics

Connection-Maker

20–30+ minutes

Moderate

Several years ago I was asked to help a manufacturing client create a portfolio of new products and service concepts to help them grow their floor-care business. The client had been an industry leader but hadn't raised its innovation bar of late, and they were looking to this project to re-energize their product portfolio and their personnel. Our team was a large one composed of representatives of key areas in the company—including marketing, R&D, and sales.

I often get ideas for my work while I'm working out at the gym, and the inspiration for this exercise came on the treadmill as I happened to catch a crazy little bit on the TV above me. Fitness guru Jack LaLanne, then in his late 80s, was demonstrating how one could exercise while doing household chores, including vacuuming!

I wrote to Jack and Elaine to ask for permission to show the video clip at my session and they graciously agreed. I asked my client team to have their products and a range of their competitors' vacuums and floor cleaners at the session. We brought bags of dirt and set up stations around our meeting room for small teams of clients to "work out" with the various machines and put them to the test.

An examination of competitive products is something that should be done on a regular basis, but sometimes this task is just left to the product development team within a company, and not seen in a fun, engaging way.

This exercise proved a breakthrough for my clients! It helped them see their competitors' products from different perspectives, viewing strengths and weaknesses, and led them to identify platforms and new product ideas.

Team Size:	groups of any size
Materials Needed:	competitive products, a large enough space in which to work in a dynamic fashion, the ability to move from station to station, several tables for the products

How to Do It

I've run *Competitive Products Olympics* for a variety of client projects. They are not difficult to do, but require organization and prep time. I will often ask client team members to bring products with them.

The instructions for engaging with the products will vary greatly, but the basic tips are:

Look closely at the competitive products, one product at a time, as if you have never seen this item before. Pay attention with all of your senses. How does the product look. How does it "feel" in the hand? What does it sound like? Smell like?

Set up small teams to be "champions" of a competitor's product and put each product to the test to see if it does what it purports to do. Have teams compete with each other, "showing off" the merits of their products.

You might want to add an element of music and loud cheering to this activity.

Be sure to give participants time to make notes of what they observed and learned and capture opportunities and ideas that are triggered by the exercise.

Your Experiments and Notes

Blindfolded Sensory Experience
(handwashing)

**Connection-Maker,
Idea Developer**

15+ minutes

Moderate

Several years ago I was asked to run a series of innovation sessions for a consumer products client who enjoyed working in beautiful condo settings. Our task on this occasion was to help them create a communication strategy for a line of body soaps. I noticed that our work venue, a large condo, had two bathrooms, a kitchen and a bar with a total of four sinks. The environment was certainly the inspiration for the exercise. But with some pre-planning you can do this in a less glamorous setting by bringing bowls, water, and hand towels with you to your venue. The point of this exercise is not necessarily hand washing, but it is an example of a sensory experience, that can elevate the level of insights and ideas you create with your team. The exercise is most appropriate for products or services that have a particular sensory component whether touch, texture, taste, or aroma.

This activity requires a degree of trust. I advise doing it with a client team with whom you have a mutually trusting relationship. If it's a new client, do this later in the session, after you have proven that your exercises lead to productive outcomes.

Set Up Time:	about 3 minutes
Run Time:	10+ minutes
Sharing:	1–2 minutes per team
Team Size:	6–12 people, depending on the team and the venue
Materials Needed:	depends on what you are trying to experience through senses other than sight, e.g., water, towels, blindfolds, or scarves

How to Do It

Set up pair teams. Here's the way I would direct the exercise:

We're going to do something fun and different from what you would do in your office, and you will get new learning and ideas from it. Is everyone game? Identify which person in your team will be A and who will be B. The As will now gently put these scarves or blindfolds over the eyes of the Bs. I'm watching; everyone is safe! (*Chuckle!*) The As are going to wash the hands of the Bs.

Of course, if this were a project for a hand moisturizer, for example, the instruction would be different.

Because the Bs can't see, they get to feel and experience this process. Try not to talk now about what you are thinking or feeling, just communicate if something is essential. The As might ask if the water is the right temperature. Enjoy the experience for a minute. Dry your partner's hands, take off the blindfolds and exchange the favor. At the end of the hand-washing, take your seats and jot down whatever you experienced, what you noticed with your various senses, and what you felt. Then we will go around the room and ask you to talk about the experience and see where that might lead us in terms of new ideas.

Your Experiments and Notes

Reincarnation (personal analogy)

I was first exposed to this when Synectics trained me in their method of creative problem solving. I've since done the exercise hundreds of times with client teams and with consumer participants and have done so many improvisations on it that I'm sure this version is different from what I initially learned. I view this as a poetic and meditative activity. It's definitely not the first thing to do with a team, but one to introduce when you have participants' trust. It can provide rich imagery and language to fuel new product or positioning work.

Connection-Maker

10 minutes

Moderate

When I used the exercise with consumer groups in a project to reposition a line of seasoned rice vinegars, I invited the back-room client listeners to do the exercise themselves, as I directed the respondents. The (clients') *ahas!* were audible, and the results clearly shaped new advertising.

Set Up Time:	2 minutes
Run Time:	5+ minutes
Sharing:	30 seconds to 1 minute per person
Team Size:	you can do this with groups of any size
Materials Needed:	paper and pen for each participant

How to Do It

Because this is a quiet, reflective exercise, I begin with asking participants to close their eyes and take some slow, relaxing breaths. I then give these directions, which you will vary depending upon the task you are working on. Use this script as a starting point and improvise the questions!

> For the next few minutes I am going to ask you to become _____ (*for example, a drop of golden rice vinegar*). Now what I mean is for you to actually imagine that you are a drop of vinegar; you are not a person looking at a drop of vinegar—isn't that wild? So just stay with that image and feeling for a few moments and jot down some words or whatever comes to your mind as I suggest a few questions. We'll gather your thoughts at the end.
>
> As a drop of rice vinegar . . .
>
> What do you look like?

What do you smell like?

Do you have a sound?

Who are your best buddies?

What most delights you about being this _____ (drop of vinegar)?

What turns you off?

You have a 3 word vocabulary, what do you say?

Give participants about 30 seconds in between each question to write down associations or responses. Then you can ask them to share aloud what they have written so that everyone has the opportunity to use the images and raw material as fodder for connections and ideas. Or ask them to look over their own notes and work independently to create connections or ideas against the task you are working on. If the latter, when you do ask participants to talk about their ideas, you will likely have to remind them that you don't want to hear all the images and associations that led to the ideas, but just the ideas; otherwise you will spend twice as much time fielding the exercise.

Your Experiments and Notes

Kitchen Magic

This is a great exercise to do with a client team if you are comfortable in the world of food. It's not difficult to execute, but it requires thoughtful planning and preparation.

I began doing these types of kitchen experiments in my "Creating the Creative Cook Workshops" and I've found that for a client project related to new food concepts it is a remarkably successful, exciting tool in my facilitator's repertoire.

I'll describe how we did this for a client who was interested in creating a portfolio of new chocolate and confectionery items, which should give you a model that you can apply to other food-related assignments.

Our team was a large one of about 20 participants representing of a mix of business functions including marketing, consumer insights, product development (R&D), and packaging. We were fortunate to be working at a venue that had a large kitchen that was part of the client's facility. A client staff member tempered pots of dark and milk chocolate for us while we were setting up the exercise.

Prep

We asked our participants to bring to the session one or two food ingredients that they thought might go well with, or *not* go well with, chocolate. They brought in many items, such as varieties of nuts, coconut, pretzels, rice cakes, crackers, cheeses, cooked grains and spices (including chili, cardamom, powdered and crystallized ginger, basil, rosemary, lavender) and many other ingredients.

I also arranged for a caterer to create trays of bite-size fruits and vegetables (yes, even things like yams, carrots, and beets) for our explorations.

Set Up Time:	depends on number of helpers and how elaborate an exercise you do
Run Time:	30 minutes; time will vary depending upon how many participants
Sharing:	30+ minutes to capture ideas
Team Size:	teams ranging from 5–25, as long as you have enough time and the right venue for everyone to participate
Materials Needed:	pre-cooked or uncooked food ingredients relevant to your topic and typical kitchen supplies including plates and utensils, toothpicks, cook tops or microwaves, refrigerator, sink, paper towels; flip charts and markers for capturing team ideas; small pads or sticky notes for individual work

How to Do It

Success is as much in the right attitude and expecting success as in the prep!

We're going to have a chance to play with food, to use all our senses to experiment and see what magic we can make using a variety of different ingredients. Some of the combinations will be surprising and delicious; others may be less so. Please approach this with an open mind and a willingness to play.

We have yummy chocolate tempering in the pots, and you see before you a wide variety of ingredients. First part of the exercise is to just quietly walk around the room and notice what we have here; look at the gorgeous array of colors, and take in the scents. We practice food safety so before you start experimenting, please wash your hands. Then try out different combinations of two or more ingredients and dip them into the chocolate. First observe quietly. Note your expectations on your little note pads; then taste and describe your experiences and see what you like or don't like. We'll capture your experiences and the ideas that emerge in about 30 minutes after everyone has had a chance to try out a variety of food combinations.

Capture the surprises and delights and also the failures. Chances are you and your team will be astounded by many unique and wonderful creations, as well as by the new product directions they might suggest. You may have to remind your team to look for the underlying principles and learning; it's not just the specific flavor combinations, but perhaps a variety of textures in one bite, or flavors that change on the tongue over time.

Your Experiments and Notes

Animal Powers

Ron and I were conducting an innovation session with educators at the Roger Williams Zoo some years ago and I noticed a variety of fantastic plastic animal masks for sale at the zoo's gift shop. I bought a dozen and put them to use in an activity with the group that afternoon. I've used the masks on many occasions since then.

There are many ways that you can work with masks (whether of animals or people). Masks provide a veil of anonymity so consider bringing them into a research situation where you suspect it might be a bit uncomfortable for participants to speak openly or comfortably. For example: Internal company personnel issues and intimate products are two places where I have successfully used the animal masks. Masks can also help people articulate aspirations, hopes, and dreams in a candid way.

Connection-Maker, Truthsayer

15+ minutes

Moderate

Set Up Time:	2 minutes
Run Time:	5+ minutes
Sharing:	1 minute or more per person
Team Size:	individuals, or groups of any size as long as you have the time
Materials Needed:	a variety of face masks; optional: a few mirrors so that people can see themselves in their selected masks

How to Do It

Spread the masks out on a table so that participants can see the choices available to them. Your specific instructions will vary depending upon your task and team. Here are suggestions to get you started.

Invite participants to select one mask . . .

. . . that they are drawn to for whatever reason.

Or . . .

. . . that represents a power or ability that they have, or wish they had.

Or . . .

. . . that represents a person or a being who could solve a problem.

After participants select their masks, ask them to put the mask on and to imagine that they are taking on the role of that character and see how they feel. Give them three to five minutes to do that. Then ask them to take the masks off and debrief the exercise as appropriate to your task. For example, you can direct them to offer perspectives, connections, new learning about themselves, ideas, etc. When Reva and I used the masks in a highly sensitive discussion with internal employees of an IT company, participants chose to leave their masks on for quite a while as they revealed deep concerns about company policies.

Variation

A "wildcard option" which may be appropriate for certain situations is to give participants a few minutes to "act out" in their masks—roaring, walking like lions, purring like pussycats, laughing like hyenas, etc. I'm sure you get the point! And then follow with your debrief and capture ideas.

Your Experiments and Notes

3D Collage

Connection-
Maker

20+ minutes

Moderate

When I was based in Boston I had a marvelous resource for "weird" materials and began to experiment using them in creative sessions, primarily with clients. The Boston Children's Museum had a recycle center where manufacturers donated odds and ends leftover from production—colored papers and plastic, wood pieces, metallic strips, soft, stretchy, rubbery tubes, NERF-like balls, and more. I would purchase a giant bag of this stuff for a few bucks. If you don't have such a resource, start collecting odds and ends and supplement with materials of different tactile or textural qualities that you can buy in a toy store or crafts shop.

The objectives of 3D collage making are:

- to bring an element of fun and relaxation to the team,
- to get participants into a child-like creative mental space where it is easy to engage the imagination and discovery,
- to promote teamwork and creative collaboration, and ultimately
- to provide raw material for ideas and connections.

Don't be shy about trying this even with executives! Over the years I've used this exercise many times with different types of client participants. For example, it was a unique source of inspiration for a group of senior engineers in Grenoble, France, where our ultimate goal was new strategies for their large-format digital print business. They literally sat on the floor of a B&B immersed in productive play. I've also done this outdoors with diverse members of an advertising agency. It's fun, and it works.

Set Up Time:	5 minutes (plus prep time of gathering materials for your exercise)
Run Time:	10–15 minutes
Sharing:	1–2 minutes per team
Team Size:	groups of any size as long as you have the time
Materials Needed:	a variety of colorful, tactile-rich materials as described above; large tables or floor space to place the collages; flip-chart paper and colored markers; camera to record the creations; background music for added ambiance

How to Do It

Place flip-chart paper on flat surfaces around your workspace or floor as the "canvas."

Set up small teams of 2-5 people at each station.

Put a basket of collage materials in the center of the room and tell participants that they can use other items if they like.

Now we're going to have a little fun and I guarantee this will lead to new ideas, but don't worry about that for now. Come up to this resource basket and pull out a bunch of different materials that you like. Then you will have _____ (~10) minutes in your teams to create a collage that _____ (*you can keep the instruction entirely open, or focus it toward your assignment*) in some way captures the essence of _____ (*e.g., what it's like to clean the bathroom*).

Let the teams proceed to play as you roam the room and make gentle interventions if necessary. As they collect materials and create the collages, tell them they don't have to glue the items down on the paper. Chances are they will be too awkward to transport after the session, but do take photographs before you disassemble them.

There will be different ways in which you can use the collages toward your end goal. My preferred method is to have the whole group move from station to station and ask each collage creation team to present their work, inviting everyone as they listen to jot down notes and ideas towards the task. After all the teams have presented their collages, then go back and chart up connections and ideas.

Your Experiments and Notes

Additional Connection-Maker Experiments and Observations

Idea Developers

Remember the song, "Turn, Turn, Turn (to Everything There Is a Season)," adapted from the *Book of Ecclesiastes* and put to music by Pete Seeger in 1959? It became a big hit when the Byrds covered it in 1965 and it holds the record as the Number 1 song with the oldest lyrics. Here are the first lines, in case you are not familiar with "Turn, Turn, Turn."

To Everything (turn, turn, turn)
There is a season (turn, turn, turn)
And a time to every purpose, under heaven

A time to be born, a time to die
A time to plant, a time to reap
A time to kill, a time to heal
A time to laugh, a time to weep

To Everything (turn, turn, turn)
There is a season (turn, turn, turn)
And a time to every purpose, under heaven

The song is a balm for dealing with life's cycles and it has a neat parallel in the innovation work that we do. When we are tasked with designing an innovation session (or to use the colloquial, "ideation session") there is a time to generate, a time to evaluate, a time to develop. These have to be three separate and distinct steps.

Why? Because otherwise it's too tempting to merge evaluation with generation, and innovation cannot survive in a prematurely critical environment. Ideas need to be free flowing, without censorship, at least for a while so that newness, distinctiveness, and perhaps true breakthroughs can emerge. Then critique and evaluation can come into play.

The typical road map that I employ when designing an innovation meeting for a client is likely to have the following eight steps:

Activities to add more detail to selected beginning ideas and directions

1. **Grounding.** Provide pre-meeting "homework" and in-session information sharing to acquaint participants with relevant background material and clarify the objectives and purpose of the gathering.

2. **Broad Idea Generation.** Create (without critique) an array of "seeds" or beginning ideas using a variety of creative stimuli, as appropriate to the task.

3. **Focused Ideation.** Generate preliminary ideas within certain parameters or elements of the overall meeting task or objectives, still using creative stimuli as appropriate.

4. **Selection.** Identify some of these beginning ideas that fit a loose criteria screen, to develop further. At this point, criteria may be general "appeal," "intrigue," and a sense that the idea is "distinctive."

5. **Idea Development.** Individuals or small teams work with these selected beginning ideas to build more detail and muscle into them. While still working in a creative vein, we think through and strengthen the idea.

6. **Evaluation.** We work with a tighter screen of criteria, which may include addressing a consumer need, fit with business core competencies, manufacturing capability or feasibility within a certain timeframe, and many other elements as appropriate to the task.

7. **Idea Refinement.** Selected ideas are enhanced, modified, or transformed in light of evaluation criteria. Options and new ideas emerge as issues are framed as "how to's" to encourage creative problem solving.

8. **Action Plan.** Individuals or team members identify next steps for further development, championing or implementation of ideas.

These eight steps are really just the first round, as this whole process is typically repeated several times before something that was "just an idea" becomes a business platform or strategy, or a product or service makes its way into the marketplace.

No doubt you can see some parallels between this process and the "Turn, Turn, Turn" song as we plant seeds, experience many births, and "kill off" some ideas that just won't work when judged against important criteria. There's usually a lot of laughter (and hopefully no weeping!). during the iterative process.

Idea Development is the smallest section here, in terms of number of exercises, but just as important as the other sections, nonetheless! Idea

Development is critical for client teams to gain closure and feel satisfied that the ideas they have created were not just a feel-good exercise of "brainstorming." Rather, these are ideas that I characterize as "having muscle, wing and heart." They are ideas that have strength and emotional resonance, and clients have the passion to champion them to the next level of development.

Further development might require wordsmithing and preparation for a round of quantitative market research, or ideas may be sent over to the product development team to begin work on prototypes. Before we leave a client innovation session we ask who will be the champions to move a project forward and we create a preliminary timetable and plan for action. We get that level of commitment on the record for accountability and to honor the effort put forth by the client team.

Even with well-intentioned champions, the journey from idea to implementation is not an easy one. Ideas, when they first emerge, are fragile (think babies). They need "good parents" to provide nurturing and support along the way. These idea champions have to be willing to protect and grow the ideas, run interference and build alignment among many stakeholders in an organization. Sometimes they have to break the rules in order to accomplish this. Marketing maven Seth Godin writes beautifully of these folks—the "linchpins" who invent, lead, connect others, and make things happen. They experiment, thrive on uncertainty, and turn their work into art.[1]

1. Seth Godin, *Linchpin: Are You Indispensable?* Portfolio, 2010

Sometimes in spite of all the excellent work, ideas don't come to fruition. Business priorities change. Ideas that initially seemed exciting and a good fit may turn out to be ahead of their time for marketplace acceptance. Ideas that fill a consumer need can prove too expensive to produce. Or project champions are reassigned and promising ideas are never given full opportunity when handed off to others who are less invested in the outcome. It's a loss when good ideas languish in dusty reports and old computer files. For these reasons and others we urge clients to keep an "Idea Bank" that can be available to a wider audience within a firm than just those authoring the initial project. We encourage client teams to periodically revisit the Idea Bank to see if time, technology, and consumer need might be more aptly aligned to warrant retesting or building upon a nugget of the initial idea.

In similar fashion, I hope you will consider this book akin to your personal Idea Bank. Withdraw and use exercises as they fit your needs. Deposit your builds, your experiments, experiences, and new ideas in the worksheets throughout.

Haiku

I remember vividly the first time I used this exercise. Reva and I were working with a food client who had completed a massive segmentation study. We were invited in to conduct a series of qualitative sessions to bring more life and richness to the client's understanding of its target consumers. After conducting a number of qualitative groups we brought the whole client team together for an in-depth debrief and idea building process. We had amassed a tremendous amount of insights and were looking for ways to synthesize and distill them so that they would be useful to the team in a variety of efforts going forward. My illustrator, Harvey, was also in the session, creating posters that depicted each of the consumer segments.

Idea Developer

20–30 minutes

Moderate

As a final step in crystallizing our thinking about each segment, the notion of creating haiku came to me. I asked the team if they would be willing to experiment, and I reminded them of the format for haiku, a Japanese form of poetry. The English translation of the form is 17 syllables, written in 3 phrases of 5 syllables, 7 syllables, and 5 syllables; "free form" haiku is a pattern of short, long, and short statements.

The results of the experiment were exciting! The poetry is alive today in posters gracing our clients' office walls. Here's an example:

Fuel me up now, please!
Make it easy, fast and cheap
Be on my radar.

A Variation on this Exercise:

Instruct your team to create Tweets condensing ideas into 140 characters or less. This is great for brevity, but may lose the poetic nature of the experience.

Set Up Time:	3 minutes
Run Time:	20+ minutes
Sharing:	1 minute per team
Team Size:	groups of any size, working as pair teams
Materials Needed:	paper and pen or pencil for each participant

How to Do It

Use this after you have already identified many insights and created ideas. This will help in selecting, synthesizing, and crystallizing the ideas that team members find most compelling.

Ask participants to partner with another person, preferably someone from another discipline. Remind them of the haiku format. Invite them to look through the insights and ideas discussed. Select those ideas that seem most important in moving forward and create one or more haiku in each partner team.

Scan the room to see how well teams are progressing and give them a warning a minute or two before you want to stop this phase of the exercise. Then ask the teams to present their haiku and invite comments, observations, or suggestions from the full team to fine-tune the haiku.

Your Experiments and Notes

Mouthfeel

This is a great exercise if you are working with a client on a name generation project. Getting the "feel" for a name by saying it out loud is particularly important now as companies struggle to find names that can be trademarked. Many firms try eliminating vowels, or using symbols in a name, which may look pretty cool, but leave people in a quandary as to how to pronounce it.

Idea Developer

15–20 minutes

Moderate

The impetus for this exercise was a re-branding assignment for a green energy company that Lisa and I were working with. We had come up with hundreds of name candidates through a variety of creative exercises and had narrowed the list down to a top dozen. I find that good names are "tasty" on the tongue as well as to the eye and brain. I created a quick role-playing exercise on the spot to help us develop and refine the best name options. The experience quickly revealed which names to consider further, and helped with finding the right language for rebranding the company. It also provided important insights into our team's primary decision-makers' and stakeholders' receptivity to the potential name change.

Set Up Time:	2 minutes
Run Time:	15+ minutes
Team Size:	6-16 people, set up in pairs or triads
Materials Needed:	imagination

How to Do It

The right business name is more than just a collection of letters that conveys an aspect of the business or benefits. The name has to be easy to pronounce and understand when communicated verbally. We're now going to set up a series of mini improvisations to see how these name candidates might play out in the real world. I'm going to ask you to arrange yourself in pair teams or triads. Select the two name candidates from our short list that you think are the strongest based on the criteria we've already discussed. Then I will ask you to come up to the front of the group and "act out" a name in conversation, and the rest of us will listen and observe.

As moderator/facilitator, give each team a different scene, such as:

- on the phone with a prospect
- on the phone with a client of the company

- in an elevator with a stranger describing what the company does
- at home talking to a spouse
- at home talking with the kids about your work
- at a conference talking with a competitor
- at a business meeting talking with a colleague
- at a friend's home talking with someone who knows nothing about your professional world
- on an airplane talking with an interested stranger

Call upon pair teams or triads to come up to the front of the room. Give them the situation and 30 seconds to decide who is in what role. Have them spontaneously talk or act it out. Give them the option of doing one or two role-plays. Each role-play should be no more than 2 minutes.

After several teams have done their improvs, debrief the exercise to gather observations and feelings about the name candidates and "build" or generate more names if needed.

Your Experiments and Notes

Billboards

A simplified format for concept development with consumer teams

This is an exercise designed to put ideas together that I've used effectively with consumers on numerous occasions. I'll illustrate it here with a project for a client in the casual dining arena, but you can apply the principles for most product or service categories. This client wanted to get consumer feedback to a number of new menu prototypes and we were holding groups at a facility with a cadre of chefs standing by. Prototypes were brought out one at a time for us to taste and give feedback. Toward the end of the group, I asked the participants to reflect on what they had sampled and discussed, to identify their favorite and write up a "billboard" ad about it. A billboard is usually a simplified ad, designed to be able to take in quickly as you are on the move in a vehicle or walking.

Idea Developers

12–15 minutes

Moderate

Set Up Time:	1 minute
Run Time:	10–15 minutes
Sharing:	1 minute per person or team
Team Size:	groups of 6–12 working in pair teams or independently
Materials Needed:	flip-chart paper and marker for each participant or team

How to Do It

We've been covering a lot of territory here and now we want to come to our final recommendations for which of these products is the best one to _____ (*in this example, bring to the menu of this restaurant*). Working individually or in pair teams I will give you _____ (*about 8*) minutes to create a billboard ad announcing your selected new _____(*menu item*).

Your billboard should include:

- a very brief headline
- a sketch or a short sentence describing the situation or what a person might be "craving" in this _____(*menu item*)
- "announcing" this new _____(*menu item*), with a brief description of what it is and how it can be enjoyed
- a final concise tag line

We don't expect you to be copywriters or artists here, just give us your best thinking and have fun with it!

Option

If you feel that your consumer team is creative in terms of their participation thus far, make this an individual exercise. If you think they might be shy or uncomfortable doing the exercise on their own, let them pick a partner to work with. Listen and watch while they are working so you can judge the time and give them a warning about a minute before you want to call a stop. Then ask them to present their creations, and probe if you want to hear more about their thinking.

Tip

It helps to chart the format up—and of course your format will vary depending on your topic.

My experience with exercises of this nature is that about a third of the outputs will be outstanding. A third will be good and a few will be less so. Whether or not these lead directly to a client's advertising or messaging strategy, the exercise is useful because it provides closure to a discussion and clarity around which ideas are having most traction with consumers.

Your Experiments and Notes

"Concept" Templates
(for working with client teams)

When I conduct a client team Innovation Session, I will allocate 30 percent of our total session time to the development phase, from selection to action plan. We choose from among our portfolio of "preliminary" ideas the ones that seem most appealing and warrant further development. We want to add sufficient detail to these selected preliminary ideas to see whether they might be worth advancing through increasing stages of rigor, development, testing, refinement, and potentially to make their way to the marketplace. The process from conceptualization to marketplace is long and complex.

To help "dimensionalize" these beginning ideas to be clear enough in team-members' minds to evaluate them, I typically craft a concept or idea template that contains the key questions or areas for the team members to focus their creative muscle and powerful thoughts. The template components vary depending upon the nature of the assignment.

Here are two models to get you started in creating your own
For a consumer-oriented new product concept assignment:

- **Concept Code Name.** A few words that identify the essence of the idea, in a memorable way.

- **Product Description.** What it is, how it works, ingredients, whatever is relevant.

- **Consumer Benefits.** Tangible or functional benefits of the product, and Emotional Benefits—how will the consumer feel using this product.

- **Unique Position.** What is unique or distinctive about this product idea vs. what is already in the marketplace?

- **Other, as relevant.** For example, pricing, packaging might be important to flag here.

- **Unknowns or areas to investigate.** For example, perhaps this idea requires a new technology or a unique ingredient.

- **Next Steps.** If this idea is going to be pursued further, what are the critical next steps, beyond standard operating procedures?

- **A Drawing.** If possible, or use words that describe in more detail what the product might look like.

For an assignment in which we were brainstorming potential claims or benefits of a new or existing product—essentially a positioning challenge:

- **Code Name,** a few words that identify the essence of the idea, in a memorable way.
- **Compelling Headline or Claim Statement**
- **Why is this important to consumers?** Describe the consumer need, functional and emotional benefits.
- **How can the claim be supported?**
- **How can we test/prove/demonstrate the claim?**
- **How is this distinctive vs. competition?**
- **What would we want to show visually?** Include a sketch if possible.
- **Other,** as appropriate to the concept

Set Up Time:	varies, involves selection or assignment of beginning ideas to develop further
Run Time:	minimum time to allocate is 10 minutes; depending on the complexity of the project and the amount of time available for the session, you might wish to give individuals or teams 30 to 45 minutes to think through and write up one or more concepts, using a template
Sharing:	It's important to have time for concept writers to be able to present their work to the full group, and if possible to have time for team members to build on the ideas: ask questions or identify issues that will require further problem solving. Ideally your session design will include at least five minutes for sharing and building per concept.
Team Size:	small to medium size groups, with concept writing performed by individuals or small teams of 2–4
Materials Needed:	wide variety of preliminary ideas from which individuals or teams can select, or the client team leader can assign to develop further; paper and pen or pencil for each participant, or flip charts and markers

How to Do It

The broad directions are:

- Explain that team members will now be developing some of the most "appealing" (intriguing or relevant or appropriate) ideas further. This is still an opportunity for creative thinking, but the focus is on weaving in more critical thinking and business expertise to turn the starting points into clear ideas that can be evaluated and, if warranted, taken further in the development and research journey.

- Consult with your client team leader ahead of time to determine if you want participants to be assigned areas to work on, or if you want to have an entirely democratic selection process.

- When you have your short list of beginning ideas for team members to develop, determine if you want participants to work independently, in pair teams, or teams of up to four people each to think through and write up the concepts. The benefit to working individually is that participants can focus on those ideas that they have most passion for. The benefit to working in small teams is the ability to bounce ideas off of each other and draw upon a wider range of expertise.

- Give participants enough time to do the job. Circulate among them as they are working to monitor progress; you may need to adjust your time depending on their progress. Give them a five-minute warning before you are ready to bring them all together.

- When the team is reassembled, have concept writers present their ideas to the full group. Invite the listeners to improve (or build on) the ideas, or raise any questions or potential issues that the concept writers may not have envisioned. It helps if the issues are framed as "how to . . . ," to invite problem solving from the whole team.

Note

Please see Concept Format 101 (page 114) for the typical next step in developing concepts for qualitative or quantitative testing.

Your Experiments and Notes

Concept Format 101
(preparing concepts for concept testing)

Most of the companies we work with will at some point want to craft ideas into a format that can be used in qualitative or quantitative research concept testing. These concepts are typically a blend of product and positioning ideas. In general, a marketing concept describes a product (service idea or invention), how this product (service or invention) will make a consumer's (customer's, shopper's, user's) life better, and provides a strong reason to believe this is so.

Here is a widely used format:

Name of Product in a Headline

Subhead benefit statement

Body copy, which contains the following:

- **Accepted Consumer Belief (ACB).** This is the consumer insight—the problem, situation or need that a target consumer faces. It can be a perception, habit, or belief that a marketer is trying to build, change, or reinforce. This statement is often written in consumer language in the "I" context.

- **Introducing** _____ (*the Product*)

- **Description of Key Consumer Benefit.** The Benefit is the promise that the new product will resolve the problem stated in the ACB. It should be single-minded and distinctive.

- **Reasons to Believe (RTB).** These are the product details that support the benefit. They can include special product features, ingredients, endorsements, and heritage.

- **Re-statement or Summary** in a positive manner

- **Other information** including pricing, packaging, and sometimes an accompanying visual image.

Concept writing is actually quite challenging. It can take hours, if not days, to craft precisely the right words—not too many and not too few—to portray an idea in a way that allows you to get a clear read on its merits from consumers or would-be buyers. Common pitfalls are including too many elements, like a laundry list of benefits, so that the concept is confusing. Some concept writers try to turn this exercise into advertising and incorporate an array of adjectives and "fluff" into the concept. Again that confuses the issue and makes it difficult to learn what is really resonating with potential buyers or consumers of the product.

It is for these reasons that we prefer to use the more simplified Concept Templates or Billboards that we have included in this section and leave the "final" concept writing to individuals or a core team of concept writing experts.

Your Experiments and Notes

Additional Idea Developer Experiments and Observations

About the Author

It probably started in the womb of a mother who loved listening to opera, going to Broadway theater, dabbling in oil painting, and cooking delicious foods. Laurie grew up in a household where creativity was cherished and nurtured, so there was little doubt that she would craft a professional life that would integrate the arts and her personal passions. While genetics and family encouragement played a critical role, good fortune and wonderful business mentors made their mark on a career that began in direct marketing, where she was immensely grateful to learn from Stan Rapp and Tom Collins, and was given latitude to be an "intrapreneur" before that word was even coined.

A taste of facilitating creative meetings provided by training at Synectics added new tools to Laurie's repertoire, and she joined the firm as an Associate/ Consultant for three years. She left to co-found IdeaScope Associates, and for twelve years headed up consulting for this boutique strategic visioning firm which had a staff of 25, and offices in Cambridge, MA, and San Francisco.

In 1995 she reframed her professional world, launching Practical Imagination Enterprises (PIE), an Innovation and Qualitative Research Consultancy with a network of outstanding colleagues. Clients come to Laurie and PIE when they need to recharge their thinking—look at their business differently, create future vision, generate and develop new strategies, new product and positioning ideas. Through the years Laurie has created and refined a well-proven process using the language of innovation and a host of face-to-face and on-line qualitative research methodologies, which engages three streams of human expertise: cross functional client teams, "thought leaders" who provide content to complement client teams' knowledge, and consumer teams to provide "raw material" in the form of insights and ideas.

Laurie has the privilege of working with some of the world's leading companies and brands in most every industry, and she has also been delighted to help smaller firms, entrepreneurs and non-profits flourish. She is an active member of the Qualitative Research Consultants Association (QRCA)—currently Co-Chair of the Philadelphia Chapter, is a Managing Editor of *QRCA VIEWS Magazine*, and is a frequent presenter at national and local QRCA Chapter conferences. She has presented widely and authored numerous articles on qualitative research, consumer trends, new product development, presentation skills, and healthy, creative cooking. Regarding the latter, she has self-published *Creating the Creative Cook: An Almost Vegetarian Cookbook for Almost Brave Cooks*, and periodically presents "Creating the Creative Cook" workshops.

Laurie is active in the arts as a singer with the Voices Chorale, an occasional storyteller, and performer with the Hunterdon Radio Theater. An avid organic vegetable gardener, she is still amazed and inspired by the magic process of planting seeds which turn into those mouth-watering juicy, ripe, homegrown tomatoes.